Other Books of Essays by the Same Author:

"Journeys to Bagdad"
Fifth printing.

"There's Pippins and Cheese to Come"
Third printing.

"Chimney-Pot Papers"
Second printing.

Also a novel, published by The Century Co.,
New York City,
"Luca Sarto"
Second printing.

Hints to Pilgrims

HINTS
TO
PILGRIMS
BY
CHARLES S. BROOKS
With Pictures by
Florence Minard

NEW HAVEN:
YALE UNIVERSITY PRESS
LONDON: HUMPHREY MILFORD
OXFORD UNIVERSITY PRESS
MDCCCCXXI

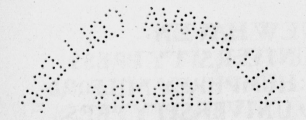

To Edward B. Greene,
as witness of our long friendship and my high regard.

Contents.

Hints to Pilgrims.

WHEN a man's thoughts in older time were set on pilgrimage, his neighbors came forward with suggestions. One of them saw that his boots were freshly tapped. Another was careful that his hose were darned with honest wool—an oldish aunt, no doubt, with beeswax and thimble and glasses forward on her nose. A third sly creature fetched in an embroidered wallet to hold an extra shift, and hinted in return for a true nail from the holy cross. If he were a bachelor, a tender garter was offered him by a lonely maiden of the village, and was acknowledged beneath the moon. But the older folk who had made the pilgrimage took the settle and fell to argument on the merit of the inns. They scrawled maps for his guidance on the hearth, and told him the sights that must not be missed. Here he must veer off for a holy well. Here he must beware a treacherous bog. Here he must ascend a steeple for the view. They cautioned him to keep upon the highway. Was it not Christian, they urged, who was lost in By-path Meadow? Again they talked of thieves and warned him to lay a chair against the door. Then a honey syllabub was drunk in clinking cups, and they made a night of it.

Or perhaps our pilgrim belonged to a guild which— by an agreeable precedent--voted that its members

walk with him to the city's gate and present from each
a half-penny to support him on the journey. The
greasy pockets yield their treasure. He rattles on
both sides with generous copper. Here, also, is a salve
for man and beast—a receipt for a fever-draught.
We may fancy now the pilgrim's mule plowing up the
lazy dust at the turn of the road as he waves his last
farewell. His thoughts already have leaped the valley
to the misty country beyond the hills.

And now above his dusty road the sun climbs the
exultant noon. It whips its flaming chariot to the
west. On the rim of twilight, like a traveler who de-
parts, it throws a golden offering to the world.

But there are pilgrims in these later days, also,—
strangers to our own fair city, script in wallet and
staff in hand,—who come to place their heavy tribute
on our shrine. And to them I offer these few suggestions.

The double stars of importance—as in Baedeker—
mark our restaurants and theatres. Dear pilgrim,
put money in thy purse! Persuade your guild to advance you to a penny! They mark the bridges, the
shipping, the sharp canyons of the lower city, the
parks—limousines where silk and lace play nurse to
lap dogs—Bufo on an airing, the precious spitz upon
a scarlet cushion. They mark the parade of wealth,
the shops and glitter of Fifth Avenue on a winter
afternoon. "If this is Fifth Avenue,"—as I heard a
dazzled stranger comment lately on a bus-top,—"my
God! what must First Avenue be like!"

And then there are the electric signs—the mammoth kitten rolling its ball of silk, ginger-ale that forever issues from a bottle, a fiery motor with a flame of dust, the Wrigley triplets correcting their sluggish livers by exercise alongside the Astor roof. Surely letters despatched home to Kalamazoo deal excitedly with these flashing portents. And of the railroad stations and the Woolworth Tower with its gothic pinnacles questing into heaven, what pilgrim words are adequate! Here, certainly, Kalamazoo is baffled and must halt and bite its pen.

Nor can the hotels be described—toppling structures that run up to thirty stories—at night a clatter in the basement and a clatter on the roof—sons of Belial and rich folk from Akron who are spending the profit on a few thousand hot-water bottles and inner tubes—what mad pursuit! what pipes and timbrels! what wild ecstasy! Do we set a noisy band upon our towers in the hope that our merriment will sound to Mars? Do we persuade them that jazz is the music of the spheres? But at morning in these hotels are thirty stories of snoring bipeds—exhausted trousers across the bed-post, frocks that have been rumpled in the hubbub—tier on tier of bipeds, with sleepy curtains drawn against the light. Boniface, in the olden time, sunning himself beneath his bush and swinging dragon, watching the dust for travelers, how would he be amazed at the advancement of the inn! Dear pilgrim, you must sag and clink for entrance to the

temples of our joyous gods. Put money in thy purse
and wire ahead!

On these streets there is a roar of traffic that Babylon never heard. Nineveh in its golden age could have
packed itself with all its splendid luggage in a single
building. Athens could have mustered in a street.
Our block-parties that are now the fashion—neighborhood affairs in fancy costumes, with a hot trombone,
and banners stretched from house to house—produce
as great an uproar as ever arose upon the Acropolis.
And lately, when our troops returned from overseas
and marched beneath our plaster arches, Rome itself
could not have matched the largeness of our triumph.
Here, also, men have climbed up to walls and battlements—but to what far dizzier heights!—to towers
and windows, and to chimney-tops, to see great
Pompey pass the streets.

And by what contrast shall we measure our tall
buildings? Otus and Ephialtes, who contracted once
to pile Pelion on top of Ossa, were evidently builders
who touched only the larger jobs. They did not stoop
to a cottage or a bungalow, but figured entirely on
such things as arks and the towers of Jericho. When
old Cheops sickened, it is said, and thought of death,
they offered a bid upon his pyramid. Noah, if he was
indeed their customer, as seems likely, must have
fretted them as their work went forward. Whenever
a cloud appeared in the rainy east he nagged them for
better speed. He prowled around on Sunday mornings with his cubit measure to detect any shortness in

the beam. Or he looked for knot-holes in the gopher wood. But Otus and Ephialtes could not, with all their sweating workmen, have fetched enough stones for even the foundations of one of our loftier structures.

The Tower of Babel, if set opposite Wall Street, would squat as low as Trinity: for its top, when confusion broke off the work, had advanced scarcely more than seven stories from the pavement. My own windows, dwarfed by my surroundings, look down from as great a height. Indeed, I fancy that if the famous tower were my neighbor to the rear—on Ninth Street, just off the L—its whiskered masons on the upmost platform could have scraped acquaintance with our cook. They could have gossiped at the noon hour from gutter to sink, and eaten the crullers that the kind creature tossed across. Our whistling grocery-man would have found a rival. And yet the good folk of the older Testament, ignorant of our accomplishment to come, were in amazement at the tower, and strangers came in from Gilead and Beersheba. Trippers, as it were, upon a holiday—staff in hand and pomegranates in a papyrus bag—locusts and wild honey, or manna to sustain them in the wilderness on their return—trippers, I repeat, cocked back their heads, and they counted the rows of windows to the top and went off to their far land marveling.

The Bankers Trust Building culminates in a pyramid. Where this narrows to a point there issues a streamer of smoke. I am told that inside this pyra-

mid, at a dizzy height above the street, there is a
storage room for gold. Is it too fanciful to think that
inside, upon this unsunned heap of metal, there is concealed an altar of Mammon with priests to feed the
fire, and that this smoke, rising in the lazy air, is sweet
in the nostrils of the greedy god?

There is what seems to be a chapel on the roof of
the Bush Terminal. Gothic decoration marks our
buildings—the pointed arch, mullions and gargoyles.
There are few nowadays to listen to the preaching of
the church, but its symbol is at least a pretty ornament
on our commercial towers.

Nor in the general muster of our sights must I
forget the magic view from across the river, in the end
of a winter afternoon, when the lower city is still
lighted. The clustered windows shine as if a larger
constellation of stars had met in thick convention.
But it is to the eye of one who travels in the evening
mist from Staten Island that towers of finest gossamer
arise. They are built to furnish a fantastic dream.
The architect of the summer clouds has tried here his
finer hand.

It was only lately when our ferry-boat came around
the point of Governor's Island, that I noticed how
sharply the chasm of Broadway cuts the city. It was
the twilight of a winter's day. A rack of sullen clouds
lay across the sky as if they met for mischief, and the
water was black with wind. In the threatening ob-
scurity the whole island seemed a mightier House of
Usher, intricate of many buildings, cleft by Broadway

in its middle, and ready to fall prostrate into the dark waters of the tarn. But until the gathering tempest rises and an evil moon peers through the crevice, as in the story, we must judge the city to be safe.

Northward are nests of streets, thick with children. One might think that the old woman who lived in a shoe dwelt hard by, with all of her married sisters roundabout. Children scurry under foot, oblivious of contact. They shoot their marbles between our feet, and we are the moving hazard of their score. They chalk their games upon the pavement. Baseball is played, long and thin, between the gutters. Peddlers' carts line the curb—carrots, shoes and small hardware —and there is shrill chaffering all the day. Here are dim restaurants, with truant smells for their advertisement. In one of these I was served unleavened bread. Folk from Damascus would have felt at home, and yet the shadow of the Woolworth Tower was across the roof. The loaf was rolled thin, like a chair-pad that a monstrous fat man habitually sits upon. Indeed, I looked sharply at my ample waiter on the chance that it was he who had taken his ease upon my bread. If Kalamazoo would tire for a night of the Beauty Chorus and the Wrigley triplets, and would walk these streets of foreign population, how amazing would be its letters home!

Our Greenwich Village, also, has its sights. Time was when we were really a village beyond the city. Even more remotely there were farms upon us and comfortable burghers jogged up from town to find the peace of country. There was once a swamp where Washington Square now is, and, quite lately, masons in demolishing a foundation struck into a conduit of running water that still drains our pleasant park. When Broadway was a muddy post-road, stretching for a weary week to Albany, ducks quacked about us and were shot with blunderbuss. Yes, and they were doubtless roasted, with apple-sauce upon the side. And then a hundred years went by, and the breathless city jumped to the north and left us a village in its midst.

It really is a village. The grocer gives you credit without question. Further north, where fashion shops, he would inspect you up and down with a cruel eye and ask a reference. He would linger on any patch or shiny spot to trip your credit. But here he wets his pencil and writes down the order without question. His friendly cat rubs against your bundles on the counter. The shoemaker inquires how your tapped soles are wearing. The bootblack, without lifting his eyes, knows you by the knots in your shoe-strings. I fear he beats his wife, for he has a great red nose which even prohibition has failed to cool. The little woman at the corner offers you the *Times* before you speak. The cigar man tosses you a package of Camels as you enter. Even the four-corners beyond Berea—unknown, remote, quite off the general travel—could hardly be more familiar with the preference of its oldest citizen. We need only a pump, and a pig and chickens in the street.

Our gossip is smaller than is found in cities. If we had yards and gardens we would talk across the fence on Monday like any village, with clothes-pins in our mouths, and pass our ailments down the street.

But we are crowded close, wall to wall. I see my neighbor cooking across the street. Each morning she jolts her dust-mop out of the window. I see shadows on a curtain as a family sits before the fire. A novelist is down below. By the frenzy of his fingers on the typewriter it must be a tale of great excitement. He never pauses or looks at the ceiling for a plot. At night he reads his pages to his patient wife, when they together have cleared away the dishes. In another window a girl lies abed each morning. Exactly at 7.45, after a few minutes of sleepy stretching, I see her slim legs come from the coverlet. Once she caught my eye. She stuck out her tongue. Your stockings, my dear, hang across the radiator.

We have odd characters, too, known to everybody, just as small towns have, who, in country circumstance, would whittle on the bench outside the village store. The father of a famous poet, but himself unknown except hereabouts, has his chair in the corner of a certain restaurant, and he offers wisdom and reminiscence to a coterie. He is our Johnson at the Mitre. Old M——, who lives in the Alley in what was once a hayloft—now a studio,—is known from Fourth to Twelfth Street for his Indian curry and his knowledge of the older poets. It is his pleasant custom to drop in on his friends from time to time and cook their dinner. He tosses you an ancient sonnet as he stirs the pot, or he beats time with his iron spoon to a melody of the Pathétique. He knows Shakespeare to a comma, and discourses so agreeably that the Madison Square clock fairly races up to midnight. Every morning, it is said—but I doubt the truth of this, for a gossiping lady told me—every morning until the general drouth set in, he issued from the Alley for a toddy to sustain his seventy years. Sometimes, she says, old M—— went without tie or collar on these quick excursions, yet with the manners of the Empire and a sweeping bow, if he met any lady of his acquaintance.

A famous lecturer in a fur collar sweeps by me often, with his eyes on the poetic stars. As he takes the air this sunny morning he thinks of new paradoxes to startle the ladies at his matinée. How they love to be shocked by his wicked speech! He is such a daring, handsome fellow—so like a god of ancient Greece! And of course most of us know T——, who gives a yearly dinner at an Assyrian restaurant—sixty cents a plate, with a near-beer extra from a saloon across the way. Any guest may bring a friend, but he must give ample warning in order that the table may be stretched.

The chief poet of our village wears a corduroy suit and goes without his hat, even in winter. If a comedy of his happens to be playing at a little theatre, he himself rings a bell in his favorite restaurant and makes the announcement in true Elizabethan fashion.

"Know ye, one and all, there is a conceited comedy this night—" His hair is always tousled. But, as its confusion continues from March into the quieter months, the disarrangement springs not so much from the outer tempest as from the poetic storms inside.

Then we have a kind of Peter Pan grown to shiny middle life, who makes ukuleles for a living. On any night of special celebration he is prevailed upon to mount a table and sing one of his own songs to this accompaniment. These songs tell what a merry, wicked crew we are. He sings of the artists' balls that ape the Bohemia of Paris, of our genius, our unrestraint, our scorn of all convention. What is morality but a suit to be discarded when it is old? What is life, he sings, but a mad jester with tinkling bells? Youth is brief, and when dead we're buried deep. So let's romp and drink and kiss. It is a pagan song that has lasted through the centuries. If it happens that any folk are down from the uptown hotels, Peter Pan consents to sell a ukulele between his encores. Here, my dear pilgrims, is an entertainment to be squeezed between Ziegfeld's and the Winter Garden.

You are welcome at all of our restaurants—our Samovars, the Pig and Whistle, the Three Steps Down (a crowded room, where you spill your soup as you carry it to a table, but a cheap, honest place in which to eat), the Green Witch, the Simple Simon. The food is good at all of these places. Grope your way into a basement—wherever one of our fantastic signs hangs out—or climb broken stairs into a dusty

garret—over a contractor's storage of old lumber and
bath-tubs—over the litter of the roofs—and you will
find artistic folk with flowing ties, spreading their
elbows at bare tables with unkept, dripping candles.

Here is youth that is blown hither from distant
villages—youth that was misunderstood at home—
youth that looks from its poor valley to the heights
and follows a flame across the darkness—youth whose
eyes are a window on the stars. Here also, alas, are
slim white moths about a candle. And here wrinkled
children play at life and art.

Here are radicals who plot the reformation of the
world. They hope it may come by peaceful means,
but if necessary will welcome revolution and machine-
guns. They demand free speech, but put to silence
any utterance less red than their own.

Here are seething sonneteers, playwrights bulging
with rejected manuscript, young women with bobbed
hair and with cigarettes lolling limply at their mouths.
For a cigarette, I have observed, that hangs loosely
from the teeth shows an artistic temperament, just as
in business circles a cigar that is tilted up until it
warms the nose marks a sharp commercial nature.

But business counts for little with us. Recently, to
make a purchase, I ventured of an evening into one of
our many small shops of fancy wares. Judge my em-
barrassment to see that the salesman was entertain-
ing a young lady on his knee. I was too far inside to
retreat. Presently the salesman shifted the lady to
his other knee and, brushing a lock of her hair off his

nose, asked me what I wanted. But I was unwilling to disturb his hospitality. I begged him not to lay down his pleasant burden, but rather to neglect my presence. He thanked me for my courtesy, and made his guest comfortable once more while I fumbled along the shelves. By good luck the price was marked upon my purchase. I laid down the exact change and tip-toed out.

The peddlers of our village, our street musicians, our apple men, belong to us. They may wander now and then to the outside world for a silver tribute, yet they smile at us on their return as at their truest friends. Ice creaks up the street in a little cart and trickles at the cracks. Rags and bottles go by with a familiar, jangling bell. Scissors grinders have a bell, also, with a flat, tinny sound, like a cow that forever jerks its head with flies. But it was only the other day that two fellows went by selling brooms. These were interlopers from a noisier district, and they raised up such a clamor that one would have thought that the Armistice had been signed again. The clatter was so unusual—our own merchants are of quieter voice— that a dozen of us thrust our heads from our windows. Perhaps another German government had fallen. The novelist below me put out his shaggy beard. The girl with the slim legs was craned out of the sill with excitement. My pretty neighbor below, who is im- maculate when I meet her on the stairs, was in her mob-cap.

My dear pilgrim from the West, with your ample

house and woodshed, your yard with its croquet set
and hammock between the wash-poles, you have no
notion how we are crowded on the island. Laundry
tubs are concealed beneath kitchen tables. Boxes for
clothes and linen are ambushed under our beds. Any
burglar hiding there would have to snuggle among the
moth balls. Sitting-room tables are swept of books
for dinner. Bookcases are desks. Desks are beds.
Beds are couches. Couches are—bless you! all the
furniture is at masquerade. Kitchen chairs turn up-
side down and become step-ladders. If anything does
not serve at least two uses it is a slacker. Beds tumble
out of closets. Fire escapes are nurseries. A patch
of roof is a pleasant garden. A bathroom becomes a
kitchen, with a lid upon the tub for groceries, and the
milk cooling below with the cold faucet drawn.

A room's use changes with the clock. That girl
who lives opposite, when she is dressed in the morning, puts a Bagdad stripe across her couch. She
punches a row of colored pillows against the wall.
Her bedroom is now ready for callers. It was only
the other day that I read of a new invention by which
a single room becomes four rooms simply by pressing
a button. This is the manner of the magic. In a
corner, let us say, of a rectangular room there is set
into the floor a turntable ten feet across. On this are
built four compartments, shaped like pieces of pie. In
one of these is placed a bath-tub and stand, in another
a folding-bed and wardrobe, in a third is a kitchen
range and cupboard, and in the fourth a bookcase and

piano. Must I explain the mystery? On rising you fold away your bed and spin the circle for your tub. And then in turn your stove appears. At last, when you have whirled your dishes to retirement, the piano comes in sight. It is as easy as spinning the caster for the oil and vinegar. A whirling Susan on the supper table is not more nimble. With this device it is estimated that the population of our snug island can be quadruplicated, and that landlords can double their rents with untroubled conscience. Or, by swinging a fifth piece of pie out of the window, a sleeping-porch could be added. When the morning alarm goes off you have only to spin the disk and dress in comfort beside the radiator. Or you could—but possibilities are countless.

Tom Paine died on Grove Street. O. Henry lived on Irving Place and ate at Allaire's on Third Avenue. The Aquarium was once a fort on an island in the river. Later Lafayette was welcomed there. And Jenny Lind sang there. John Masefield swept out a saloon, it's said, on Sixth Avenue near the Jefferson Market, and, for all I know, his very broom may be still standing behind the door. The Bowery was once a post-road up toward Boston. In the stream that flowed down Maiden Lane, Dutch girls did the family washing. In William Street, not long ago, they were tearing down the house in which Alexander Hamilton lived. These are facts at random.

But Captain Kidd lived at 119 Pearl Street. Dear me, I had thought that he was a creature of a nursery book—one of the pirates whom Sinbad fought. And here on Pearl Street, in our own city, he was arrested and taken to hang in chains in London. A restaurant now stands at 119. A bucket of oyster shells is at the door, and, inside, a clatter of hungry spoons.

But the crowd thickens on these narrow streets. Work is done for the day and tired folk hurry home. Crowds flow into the subway entrances. The streets are flushed, as it were, with people, and the flood drains to the rushing sewers. Now the lights go out one by one. The great buildings, that glistened but a moment since at every window, are now dark cliffs above us in the wintry mist.

It is time, dear pilgrim, to seek your hotel or favorite cabaret.

The Wrigley triplets once more correct by exercise their sluggish livers. The kitten rolls its ball of fiery silk. Times Square flashes with entertainment. It stretches its glittering web across the night.

Dear pilgrim, a last important word! Put money in thy purse!

I Plan a Vacation.

IT is my hope, when the snow is off the ground and the ocean has been tamed by breezes from the south, to cross to England. Already I fancy myself seated in the pleasant office of the steamship agent, listening to his gossip of rates and sailings, bending over his colored charts, weighing the merit of cabins. Here is one amidships in a location of greatest ease upon the stomach. Here is one with a forward port that will catch the sharp and wholesome wind from the Atlantic. I trace the giant funnels from deck to deck. My finger follows delightedly the confusing passages. I smell the rubber on the landings and the salty rugs. From on top I hear the wind in the cordage. I view the moon, and I see the mast swinging among the stars.

Then, also, at the agent's, for my pleasure, there is a picture of a ship cut down the middle, showing its inner furnishing and the hum of life on its many decks. I study its flights of steps, its strange tubes and vents and boilers. Munchausen's horse, when its rearward end was snapped off by the falling gate (the faithful animal, you may recall, galloped for a mile upon its forward legs alone before the misadventure was discovered)—Munchausen's horse, I insist,—the unbroken, forward half,— did not display so frankly its confusing pipes and coils. Then there is another ship which, by a monstrous effort of the printer, is laid in Broadway, where its stacks out-top Trinity. I pace its mighty length on the street before my house, and my eye climbs our tallest tree for a just comparison.

It is my hope to find a man of like ambition and endurance as myself and to walk through England. He must be able, if necessary, to keep to the road for twenty-five miles a day, or, if the inn runs before us in the dark, to stretch to thirty. But he should be a creature, also, who is content to doze in meditation beneath a hedge, heedless whether the sun, in faster boots, puts into lodging first. Careless of the hour, he may remark in my sleepy ear "how the shadows lengthen as the sun declines."

He must be able to jest when his feet are tired. His drooping grunt must be spiced with humor. When stiffness cracks him in the morning, he can the better play the clown. He will not grumble at his bed or poke too shrewdly at his food. Neither will he talk of graves and rheumatism when a rainstorm finds us unprepared. If he snuffle at the nose, he must snuffle cheerfully and with hope. Wit, with its unexpected turns, is to be desired; but a pleasant and even humor is a better comrade on a dusty road. It endures blisters and an empty stomach. A pack rests more lightly on its weary shoulders. If he sing, he should know a round of tunes and not wear a single melody to tatters. The merriest lilt grows dull and lame when it travels all the day. But although I wish my companion to be of a cheerful temper, he need not pipe or dance until the mists have left the hills. Does not the shining sun itself rise slowly to its noonday glory? A companion must give me leave to enjoy in silence my sullen breakfast.

A talent for sketching shall be welcome. Let him produce his pencils and his tablet at a pointed arch or mullioned window, or catch us in absurd posture as we travel. If one tumbles in a ditch, it is but decency to hold the pose until the picture's made.

But, chiefly, a companion should be quick with a smile and nod, apt for conversation along the road. Neither beard nor ringlet must snub his agreeable advance. Such a fellow stirs up a mixed acquaintance between town and town, to point the shortest way—a bit of modest gingham mixing a pudding at a pantry window, age hobbling to the gate on its friendly crutch, to show how a better path climbs across the hills. Or in a taproom he buys a round of ale and becomes a crony of the place. He enlists a dozen friends to sniff outdoors at bedtime, with conflicting prophecy of a shifting wind and the chance of rain.

A companion should be alert for small adventure. He need not, therefore, to prove himself, run to grapple with an angry dog. Rather, let him soothe the snarling creature! Let him hold the beast in parley while I go on to safety with unsoiled dignity! Only when arbitration and soft terms fail shall he offer a haunch of his own fair flesh. Generously he must boost me up a tree, before he seeks safety for himself.

But many a trivial mishap, if followed with a willing heart, leads to comedy and is a jest thereafter. I know a man who, merely by following an inquisitive nose through a doorway marked "No Admittance," became comrade to a company of traveling actors. The play was *Uncle Tom's Cabin,* and they were at rehearsal. Presently, at a changing of the scene, my friend boasted to Little Eva, as they sat together on a pile of waves, that he performed upon the tuba. It seems that she had previously mounted into heaven in the final picture without any welcoming trumpet of the angels. That night, by her persuasion, my friend sat in the upper wings and dispensed flutings of great joy as she ascended to her rest.

Three other men of my acquaintance were caught once, between towns, on a walking trip in the Adirondacks, and fell by chance into a kind of sanitarium for convalescent consumptives. At first it seemed a gloomy prospect. But, learning that there was a movie in a near-by village, they secured two jitneys and gave a party for the inmates. In the church parlor, when the show was done, they ate ice-cream and layer-cake. Two of the men were fat, but the third, a slight and handsome fellow—I write on suspicion only—so won a pretty patient at the feast, that, on the homeward ride—they were rattling in the tonneau—she graciously permitted him to steady her at the bumps and sudden turns.

Nor was this the end. As it still lacked an hour of midnight the general sanitarium declared a Roman holiday. The slight fellow, on a challenge, did a hand-stand, with his feet waving against the wall, while his knife and keys and money dropped from his pockets. The pretty patient read aloud some verses of her own upon the spring. She brought down her water-colors, and laying a charcoal portrait off the piano, she ranged her lovely wares upon the top. The fattest of my friends, also, eager to do his part, stretched himself, heels and head, between two chairs. But, when another chair was tossed on his unsupported middle, he fell with a boom upon the carpet. Then the old doctor brought out wine and Bohemian glasses with long stems and, as the clock struck. twelve, the company pledged one another's health, with hopes for a reunion. They lighted their candles on the landing, and so to bed.

I know a man, also, who once met a sword-swallower at a county fair. A volunteer was needed for his trick—someone to hold the scarlet cushion with its dangerous knives—and zealous friends pushed him from his seat and toward the stage. Afterwards he met the Caucasian Beauties and, despite his timidity, they dined together with great merriment.

Then there is a kind of humorous philosophy to be desired on an excursion. It smokes a contented pipe to the tune of every rivulet. It rests a peaceful stomach on the rail of every bridge, and it observes the floating leaves, like golden caravels upon the stream. It interprets a trivial event. It is both serious and absurd. It sits on a fence to moralize on

the life of cows and flings in Plato on the soul. It
plays catch and toss with life and death and the world
beyond. And it sees significance in common things.
A farmer's cart is a tumbril of the Revolution. A
crowing rooster is Chanticleer. It is the very cock
that proclaimed to Hamlet that the dawn was nigh.
When a cloud rises up, such a philosopher discourses
of the flood. He counts up the forty rainy days and
names the present rascals to be drowned—profiteers
in food, plumbers and all laundrymen.

A stable lantern, swinging in the dark, rouses up a
race of giants—

I think it was some such fantastic quality of thought
that Horace Walpole had in mind when he com-
mended the Three Princes of Serendip. Their High-
nesses, it seems, "were always making discoveries, by
accident and sagacity, of things which they were not in
quest of: for instance," he writes, "one of them discovered that a mule blind of the right eye had
traveled the same road lately, because the grass was
eaten on the left side." At first, I confess, this employment seems a waste of time. Sherlock Holmes
did better when he pronounced, on finding a neglected
whisp of beard, that Doctor Watson's shaving mirror
had been shifted to an opposite window. But doubtless the Princes put their deduction to higher use, and
met the countryside and village with shrewd and vivid
observation.

Don Quixote had this same quality, but with more
than a touch of madness. Did he not build up the

Lady Tolosa out of a common creature at an inn?
He sought knighthood at the hands of its stupid
keeper and watched his armor all night by the foolish
moon. He tilted against a windmill. I cannot whole-
heartedly commend the Don, but, for an afternoon,
certainly, I would prefer his company between town
and town to that of any man who carries his clanking
factory on his back.

But, also, I wish a companion of my travels to be
for the first time in England, in order that I may have
a fresh audience for my superior knowledge. In the
cathedral towns I wish to wave an instructive finger
in crypt and aisle. Here is a bit of early glass. Here
is a wall that was plastered against the plague when
the Black Prince was still alive. I shall gossip of
scholars in cord and gown, working at their rubric in
sunny cloisters. Or if I choose to talk of kings and
forgotten battles, I wish a companion ignorant but
eager for my boasting.

It was only last night that several of us discussed
vacations. Wyoming was the favorite—a ranch, with
a month on horseback in the mountains, hemlock
brouse for a bed, morning at five and wood to chop.
But a horse is to me a troubled creature. He stands
to too great a height. His eye glows with exultant
deviltry as he turns and views my imperfection. His
front teeth seem made for scraping along my arm.
I dread any fly or bee lest it sting him to emotion.
I am point to point in agreement with the psalmist:
"An horse is a vain thing for safety." If I must ride,

I demand a tired horse, who has cropped his wild oats
and has come to a slippered state. Are we not told
that the horse in the crustaceous age—I select a large
word at random—was built no bigger than a dog?
Let this snug and peerless ancestor be saddled and I
shall buy a ticket for the West.

But I do not at this time desire to beard the wilderness. There is a camp of Indians near the ranch. I
can smell them these thousand miles away. Their
beads and greasy blankets hold no charm. Smoky
bacon, indeed, I like. I can lie pleasurably at the flap
of the tent with sleepy eyes upon the stars. I can
even plunge in a chilly pool at dawn. But the Indians
and horses that infest Wyoming do not arouse my
present interest.

I am for England, therefore—for its winding roads,
its villages that nest along the streams, its peaked
bridges with salmon jumping at the weir, its thatched
cottages and flowering hedges.

> "The chaffinch sings on the orchard bough
>   In England—now!"

I wish to see reapers at work in Surrey fields, to
stride over the windy top of Devon, to cross Wiltshire
when wind and rain and mist have brought the Druids
back to Stonehenge. At a crossroad Stratford is ten
miles off. Raglan's ancient towers peep from a
wooded hill. Tintern or Glastonbury can be gained
by night. Are not these names sweet upon the
tongue? And I wish a black-timbered inn in which to

end the day—with polished brasses in the tap and the smell of the musty centuries upon the stairs.

At the window of our room the Cathedral spire rises above the roofs. There is no trolley-car or creaking of any wheel, and on the pavement we hear only the fall of feet in endless pattern. Day weaves a hurrying mesh, but this is the quiet fabric of the night.

I wish to walk from London to Inverness, to climb

the ghostly ramparts of Macbeth's castle, to hear the
shrill cry of Duncan's murder in the night, to watch
for witches on the stormy moor. I shall sit on the
bench where Johnson sat with Boswell on his journey
to the Hebrides. I shall see the wizard of the North,
lame of foot, walking in the shade of ruined Dry-
burgh. With drunken Tam, I shall behold in Allo-
way Kirk warlocks in a dance. From the gloomy
house of Shaws and its broken tower David Balfour
runs in flight across the heather. Culloden echoes with
the defeat of an outlaw prince. The stairs of Holy-
rood drip with Rizzio's blood. But also, I wish to follow the Devon lanes, to rest in villages on the coast at
the fall of day when fishermen wind their nets, to
dream of Arthur and his court on the rocks beyond
Tintagel. Merlin lies in Wales with his dusty garments pulled about him, and his magic sleeps. But
there is wind tonight in the noisy caverns of the sea,
and Spanish pirates dripping with the slime of a
watery grave, bury their treasure when the fog lies
thick.

Thousands of years have peopled these English
villages. Their pavements echo with the tread of
kings and poets. Here is a sunny bower for lovers
when the world was young. Bishops of the Roman
church—Saint Thomas himself in his robes pontifical
has walked through these broken cloisters. Here is
the altar where he knelt at prayer when his assassins
came. From that tower Mary of Scotland looked
vainly for assistance to gallop from the north.

Here stretches the Pilgrims' Way across the downs of Surrey—worn and scratched by pious feet. From the west they came to Canterbury. The wind stirs the far-off traffic, and the mist covers the hills as with an ancient memory.

How many thirsty elbows have rubbed this table in the forgotten years! How many feasts have come steaming from the kitchen when the London coach was in! That pewter cup, maybe, offered its eager pledge when the news of Agincourt was blown from France. Up that stairway Tom Jones reeled with sparkling canary at his belt. These cobbles clacked in the Pretender's flight. Here is the chair where Falstaff sat when he cried out that the sack was spoiled with villainous lime. That signboard creaked in the tempest that shattered the Armada.

My fancy mingles in the past. It hears in the inn-yard the chattering pilgrims starting on their journey. Here is the Pardoner jesting with the merry Wife of Bath, with his finger on his lips to keep their scandal private. It sees Dick Turpin at the crossroads with loaded pistols in his boots. There is mist tonight on Bagshot Heath, and men in Kendal green are out. And fancy rebuilds a ruined castle, and lights the hospitable fires beneath its mighty caldrons. It hangs tapestry on its empty walls and, like a sounding trumpet, it summons up a gaudy company in ruff and velvet to tread the forgotten measures of the past.

Let Wyoming go and hang itself in its muddy riding-boots and khaki shirt! Let its tall horses leap

upward and click their heels upon the moon! I am
for England.

It is my preference to land at Plymouth, and our
anchor—if the captain is compliant—will be dropped
at night, in order that the Devon hills, as the thrifty
stars are dimmed, may appear first through the mists
of dawn. If my memory serves, there is a country
church with stone-embattled tower on the summit
above the town, and in the early twilight all the roads
that climb the hills lead away to promised kingdoms.
Drake, I assert, still bowls nightly on the quay at
Plymouth, with pins that rattle in the windy season,
but the game is done when the light appears.

We clatter up to London. Paddington station or
Waterloo, I care not. But for arrival a rainy night is
best, when the pavements glisten and the mad taxis
are rushing to the theatres. And then, for a week, by
way of practice and to test our boots, we shall trudge
the streets of London—the Strand and the Embank-
ment. And certainly we shall explore the Temple
and find the sites of Blackfriars and the Globe. Here,
beyond this present brewery, was the bear-pit. Tarl-
ton's jests still sound upon the bank. A wherry, once,
on this busy river, conveyed Sir Roger up to Vauxhall. Perhaps, here, on the homeward trip, he was
rejected by the widow. The dear fellow, it is re-
corded, out of sentiment merely, kept his clothes unchanged in the fashion of this season of his disappoint-
ment. Here, also, was the old bridge across the Fleet.
Here was Drury Lane where Garrick acted. Tender

hearts, they say, in pit and stall, fluttered to his Romeo, and sighed their souls across the candles. On this muddy curb link-boys waited when the fog was thick. Here the footmen bawled for chairs.

But there are bookshops still in Charing Cross Road. And, for frivolous moments, haberdashery is offered in Bond Street and vaudeville in Leicester Square.

And then on a supreme morning we pack our rucksacks.

It was a grievous oversight that Christian failed to tell us what clothing he carried in his pack. We know it was a heavy burden, for it dragged him in the mire. But did he carry slippers to ease his feet at night? And what did the Pardoner put inside his wallet? Surely the Wife of Bath was supplied with a powder-puff and a fresh taffeta to wear at the journey's end. I could, indeed, spare Christian one or two of his encounters for knowledge of his wardrobe. These homely details are of interest. The mad Knight of La Mancha, we are told, mortgaged his house and laid out a pretty sum on extra shirts. Stevenson, also, tells us the exact gear that he loaded on his donkey, but what did Marco Polo carry? And Munchausen and the Wandering Jew? I have skimmed their pages vainly for a hint.

For myself, I shall take an extra suit of underwear and another flannel shirt, a pair of stockings, a rubber cape of lightest weight that falls below the knees, slippers, a shaving-kit and brushes. I shall

wash my linen at night and hang it from my window,
where it shall wave like an admiral's flag to show that
I sleep upon the premises. I shall replace it as it
wears. And I shall take a book, not to read but to
have ready on the chance. I once carried the Book
of Psalms, but it was Nick Carter I read, which I
bought in a tavern parlor, fifteen pages missing, from
a fat lady who served me beer.

We run to the window for a twentieth time. It has
rained all night, but the man in the lift was hopeful
when we came up from breakfast. We believe him; as
if he sat on a tower with a spy-glass on the clouds.
We cherish his tip as if it came from Æolus himself,
holding the winds in leash.

And now a streak of yellowish sky—London's substitute for blue—shows in the west.

We pay our bill. We scatter the usual silver.
Several senators in uniform bow us down the steps.
We hale a bus in Trafalgar Square. We climb to the
top—to the front seat with full prospect. The Hay-
market. Sandwich men with weary step announce a
vaudeville. We snap our fingers at so stale an entertainment. There are flower-girls in Piccadilly Circus.
Regent Street. We pass the Marble Arch, near
which cut-throats were once hanged on the three-
legged mare of Tyburn. Hammersmith. Brentford.
The bus stops. It is the end of the route. We have
ridden out our sixpence. We climb down. We
adjust our packs and shoe-strings. The road to the
western country beckons.

My dear sir, perhaps you yourself have planned for a landaulet this summer and an English trip. You have laid out two swift weeks to make the breathless round. You journey from London to Bristol in a day. Another day, and you will climb out, stiff of leg, among the northern lakes. If then, as you loll among the cushions, lapped in luxury, pink and soft— if then, you see two men with sticks in hand and packs on shoulder, know them for ourselves. We are singing on the road to Windsor—to Salisbury, to Stonehenge, to the hills of Dorset, to Lyme-Regis, to Exeter and the Devon moors.

It was a shepherd who came with a song to the mountain-top. "The sun shone, the bees swept past me singing; and I too sang, shouted, World, world, I am coming!"

At a Toy-Shop Window.

IN this Christmas season, when snowflakes fill the air and twilight is the pleasant thief of day, I sometimes pause at the window of a toy-shop to see what manner of toys are offered to the children. It is only five o'clock and yet the sky is dark. The night has come to town to do its shopping before the stores are shut. The wind has Christmas errands.

And there is a throng of other shoppers. Fathers of families drip with packages and puff after street cars. Fat ladies—Now then, all together!—are hoisted up. Old ladies are caught in revolving doors. And the relatives of Santa Claus—surely no nearer than nephews (anæmic fellows in faded red coats and cotton beards)—pound their kettles for an offering toward a Christmas dinner for the poor.

But, also, little children flatten their noses on the window of the toy-shop. They point their thumbs through their woolly mittens in a sharp rivalry of choice. Their unspent nickels itch for large investment. Extravagant dimes bounce around their pockets. But their ears are cold, and they jiggle on one leg against a frosty toe.

Here in the toy-shop is a tin motor-car. Here is a railroad train, with tracks and curves and switches, a pasteboard mountain and a tunnel. Here is a steamboat. With a turning of a key it starts for Honolulu behind the sofa. The stormy Straits of Madagascar lie along the narrow hall. Here in the window, also, are beams and girders for a tower. Not since the days of Babel has such a vast supply been gathered. And there are battleships and swift destroyers and guns and armoured tanks. The nursery becomes a dangerous ocean, with submarines beneath the stairs: or it is the plain of Flanders and the great war echoes across the hearth. Château-Thierry is a pattern in the rug and the andirons are the towers of threatened Paris.

But on this Christmas night, as I stand before the toy-shop in the whirling storm, the wind brings me the laughter of far-off children. Time draws back its sober curtain. The snow of thirty winters is piled in my darkened memory, but I hear shrill voices across the night.

Once upon a time—in the days when noses and tables were almost on a level, and manhood had wavered from kilts to pants buttoning at the side—

once there was a great chest which was lodged in a closet behind a sitting-room. It was from this closet that the shadows came at night, although at noon there was plainly a row of hooks with comfortable winter garments. And there were drawers and shelves to the ceiling where linen was kept, and a cupboard for cough-syrup and oily lotions for chapped hands. A fragrant paste, also, was spread on the tip of the little finger, which, when wiggled inside the nostril and inhaled, was good for wet feet and snuffles. Twice a year these bottles were smelled all round and half of them discarded. It was the ragman who bought them, a penny to the bottle. He coveted chiefly, however, lead and iron, and he thrilled to old piping as another man thrills to Brahms. He was a sly fellow and, unless Annie looked sharp, he put his knee against the scale.

But at the rear of the closet, beyond the lamplight, there was a chest where playing-blocks were kept. There were a dozen broken sets of various shapes and sizes—the deposit and remnant of many years.

These blocks had once been covered with letters and pictures. They had conspired to teach us. C had stood for cat. D announced a dog. Learning had put on, as it were, a sugar coat for pleasant swallowing. The arid heights teased us to mount by an easy slope. But we scraped away the letters and the pictures. Should a holiday, we thought, be ruined by insidious instruction? Must a teacher's wagging finger always come among us? It was sufficient that

five blocks end to end made a railway car, with finger-
blocks for platforms; that three blocks were an engine,
with a block on top to be a smokestack. We had no
toy mountain and pasteboard tunnel, as in the soft
fashion of the present, but we jacked the rug with
blocks up hill and down, and pushed our clanking
trains through the hollow underneath. It was an
added touch to build a castle on the summit. A spool
on a finger-block was the Duke himself on horseback,
hunting across his sloping acres.

There was, also, in the chest, a remnant of iron coal-
cars with real wheels. Their use was too apparent.
A best invention was to turn playthings from an
obvious design. So we placed one of the coal-cars
under the half of a folding checkerboard and by
adding masts and turrets and spools for guns we built
a battleship. This could be sailed all round the room,
on smooth seas where the floor was bare, but it pitched
and tossed upon a carpet. If it came to port battered
by the storm, should it be condemned like a ship that
is broken on a sunny river? Its plates and rivets had
been tested in a tempest. It had skirted the headlands
at the staircase and passed the windy Horn.

Or perhaps we built a fort upon the beach before
the fire. It was a pretty warfare between ship and
fort, with marbles used shot and shot in turn. A
lucky marble toppled the checkerboard off its balance
and wrecked the ship. The sailors, after scrambling
in the water, put to shore on flat blocks from the boat
deck and were held as prisoners until supper, in the

dungeons of the fort. It was in the sitting-room that
we played these games, under the family's feet. They
moved above our sport like a race of tolerant giants;
but when callers came, we were brushed to the rear of
the house.

Spools were men. Thread was their short and subsidiary use. Their larger life was given to our armies.
We had several hundred of them threaded on long
strings on the closet-hooks. But if a great campaign
was planned—if the Plains of Abraham were to be
stormed or Cornwallis captured—our recruiting ser-
geants rummaged in the drawers of the sewing-
machine for any spool that had escaped the draft. Or
we peeked into mother's work-box, and if a spool was
almost empty, we suddenly became anxious about our
buttons. Sometimes, when a great spool was needed
for a general, mother wound the thread upon a piece
of cardboard. General Grant had carried black silk.
Napoleon had been used on trouser-patches. And
my grandmother and a half-dozen aunts and elder
cousins did their bit and plied their needles for the
war. In this regard grandfather was a slacker, but
he directed the battle from the sofa with his crutch.

Toothpicks were guns. Every soldier had a gun.
If he was hit by a marble in the battle and the toothpick remained in place, he was only wounded; but he
was dead if the toothpick fell out. Of each two men
wounded, by Hague Convention, one recovered for
the next engagement.

Of course we had other toys. Lead soldiers in

cocked hats came down the chimney and were mar-
shaled in the Christmas dawn. A whole Continental
Army lay in paper sheets, to be cut out with scissors.
A steam engine with a coil of springs and key furnished several rainy holidays. A red wheel-barrow
supplied a short fury of enjoyment. There were
sleds and skates, and a printing press on which we
printed the milkman's tickets. The memory still
lingers that five cents, in those cheap days, bought a
pint of cream. There was, also, a castle with a princess at a window. Was there no prince to climb her
trellis and bear her off beneath the moon? It had
happened so in Astolat. The princes of the gorgeous
East had wooed, also, in such a fashion. Or perhaps
this was the very castle that the wicked Kazrac lifted
across the Chinese mountains in the night, cheating
Aladdin of his bride. It was a rather clever idea, as
things seem now in this time of general shortage, to
steal a lady, house and all, not forgetting the cook
and laundress. But one day a little girl with dark
hair smiled at me from next door and gave me a
Christmas cake, and in my dreams thereafter she
became the princess in my castle.

We had stone blocks with arches and round columns
that were too delicate for the hazard of siege and
battle. Once, when a playmate had scarlet fever, we
lent them to him for his convalescence. Afterwards,
against contagion, we left them for a month under a
bush in the side yard. Every afternoon we wet them
with a garden hose. Did not Noah's flood purify the

world? It would be a stout microbe, we thought, that could survive the deluge. At last we lifted out the blocks at arm's length. We smelled them for any lurking fever. They were damp to the nose and smelled like the cement under the back porch. But the contagion had vanished like Noah's wicked neighbors.

But store toys always broke. Wheels came off. Springs were snapped. Even the princess faded at her castle window.

Sometimes a toy, when it was broken, arrived at a larger usefulness. Although I would not willingly forget my velocipede in its first gay youth, my memory of sharpest pleasure reverts to its later days, when one of its rear wheels was gone. It had been jammed in an accident against the piano. It has escaped me whether the piano survived the jolt; but the velocipede was in ruins. When the wheel came off the brewery wagon before our house and the kegs rolled here and there, the wreckage was hardly so complete. Three spokes were broken and the hub was cracked. At first, it had seemed that the day of my velocipede was done. We laid it on its side and tied the hub with rags. It looked like a jaw with tooth-ache. Then we thought of the old baby-carriage in the storeroom. Perhaps a transfusion of wheels was possible. We conveyed upstairs a hammer and a saw. It was a wobbling and impossible experiment. But at the top of the house there was a kind of race-track around the four posts of the attic. With three

wheels complete, we had been forced to ride with
caution at the turns or be pitched against the sloping
rafters. We now discovered that a missing wheel
gave the necessary tilt for speed. I do not recall that
the pedals worked. We legged it on both sides. Ten
times around was a race; and the audience sat on the
ladder to the roof and held a watch with a second-
hand for records.

Ours was a roof that was flat in the center. On
winter days, when snow would pack, we pelted the
friendly milkman. Ours, also, was a cellar that was
lost in darkened mazes. A blind area off the laundry,
where the pantry had been built above, seemed to be
the opening of a cavern. And we shuddered at the
sights that must meet the candle of the furnaceman
when he closed the draught at bedtime.

Abandoned furniture had uses beyond a first in-
tention. A folding-bed of ours closed to about the
shape of a piano. When the springs and mattress
were removed it was a house with a window at the
end where a wooden flap let down. Here sat the
Prisoner of Chillon, with a clothes-line on his ankle.
A pile of old furniture in the attic, covered with a
cloth, became at twilight a range of mountains with a
gloomy valley at the back. I still believe—for so does
fancy wanton with my thoughts—that Aladdin's cave
opens beneath those walnut bed-posts, that the cavern
of jewels needs but a dusty search on hands and knees.
The old house, alas, has come to foreign use. Does no
one now climb the attic steps? Has time worn down

the awful Caucasus? No longer is there children's
laughter on the stairs. The echo of their feet sleeps at
last in the common day.

Nor must furniture, of. necessity, be discarded.
We dived from the footboard of our bed into a surf
of pillows. We climbed its headboard like a mast,
and looked for pirates on the sea. A sewing-table
with legs folded flat was a sled upon the stairs. Must
I do more than hint that two bed-slats make a pair
of stilts, and that one may tilt like King Arthur with
the wash-poles? Or who shall fix a narrow use for
the laundry tubs, or put a limit on the coal-hole? And
step-ladders! There are persons who consider a step-
ladder as a menial. This is an injustice to a giddy
creature that needs but a holiday to show its metal.
On Thursday afternoons, when the cook was out, you
would never know it for the same thin creature that
goes on work-days with a pail and cleans the windows.
It is a tower, a shining lighthouse, a crowded grand-
stand, a circus, a ladder to the moon.

But perhaps, my dear young sir, you are so lucky
as to possess a smaller and inferior brother who frets
with ridicule. He is a toy to be desired above a red
velocipede. ∴ I offer you a hint. Print upon a paper
in bold, plain letters—sucking the lead for extra
blackness—that he is afraid of the dark, that he likes
the girls, that he is a butter-fingers at baseball and
teacher's pet and otherwise contemptible. Paste the
paper inside the glass of the bookcase, so that the
insult shows. Then lock the door and hide the key.

Let him gaze at this placard of his weakness during a rainy afternoon. But I caution you to secure the keys of all similar glass doors—of the china closet, of the other bookcase, of the knick-knack cabinet. Let him stew in his iniquity without chance of retaliation.

But perhaps, in general, your brother is inclined to imitate you and be a tardy pattern of your genius. He apes your fashion in suspenders, the tilt of your cap, your method in shinny. If you crouch in a barrel in hide-and-seek, he crowds in too. You wag your head from side to side on your bicycle in the manner of Zimmerman, the champion. Your brother wags his, too. You spit in your catcher's mit, like Kelly, the ten-thousand-dollar baseball beauty. Your brother spits in his mit, too. These things are un-bearable. If you call him "sloppy" when his face is dirty, he merely passes you back the insult unchanged. If you call him "sloppy-two-times," still he has no invention. You are justified now to call him "nigger" and to cuff him to his place.

Tagging is his worst offense—tagging along behind when you are engaged on serious business. "Now then, sonny," you say, "run home. Get nurse to blow your nose." Or you bribe him with a penny to mind his business.

I must say a few words about paper-hangers, although they cannot be considered as toys or play-things by any rule of logic. There is something rather jolly about having a room papered. The removal of the pictures shows how the old paper looked before it faded. The furniture is pushed into an agreeable confusion in the hall. A rocker seems starting for the kitchen. The great couch goes out the window. A chair has climbed upon a table to look about. It needs but an alpenstock to clamber on the bookcase. The carpet marks the places where the piano legs came down.

And the paper-hanger is a rather jolly person. He sings and whistles in the empty room. He keeps to a tune, day after day, until you know it. He slaps his brush as if he liked his work. It is a sticky, splashing, sloshing slap. Not even a plasterer deals in more interesting material. And he settles down on you with ladders and planks as if a circus had moved in. After hours, when he is gone, you climb on his planking and cross Niagara, as it were, with a cane for balance. To this day I think of paper-hangers as a kindly race of men, who sing in echoing rooms and eat pie and pickles for their lunch. Except for their Adam's apples—got with gazing at the ceiling—surely not the wicked apple of the Garden—I would wish to be a paper-hanger.

Plumbers were a darker breed, who chewed tobacco fetched up from their hip-pockets. They were enemies of the cook by instinct, and they spat in dark corners. We once found a cake of their tobacco when they were gone. We carried it to the safety of the furnace-room and bit into it in turn. It was of a sweetish flavor of licorice that was not unpleasant. But the sin was too enormous for our comfort.

But in November, when days were turning cold and hands were chapped, our parents' thoughts ran to the kindling-pile, to stock it for the winter. Now the kindling-pile was the best quarry for our toys, because it was bought from a washboard factory around the corner. Not every child has the good fortune to live near a washboard factory. Necessary as washboards are, a factory of modest output can supply a county, with even a little dribble for export into neighbor counties. Many unlucky children, therefore, live a good ten miles off, and can never know the fascinating discard of its lathes—the little squares and cubes, the volutes and rhythmic flourishes which are cast off in manufacture and are sold as kindling. They think a washboard is a dull and common thing. To them it smacks of Monday. It smells of yellow soap and suds. It wears, so to speak, a checkered blouse and carries clothes-pins in its mouth. It has perspiration on its nose. They do not know, in their pitiable ignorance, the towers and bridges that can be made from the scourings of a washboard factory.

Our washboard factory was a great wooden structure that had been built for a roller-skating rink. Father and mother, as youngsters in the time of their courtship, had cut fancy eights upon the floor. And still, in these later days, if you listened outside a window, you heard a whirling roar, as if perhaps the skaters had returned and again swept the corners madly. But it was really the sound of machinery that you heard, fashioning toys and blocks for us. At noonday, comely red-faced girls ate their lunches on the window-sills, ready for conversation and acquaintance.

And now, for several days, a rumor has been running around the house that a wagon of kindling is expected. Each afternoon, on our return from school, we run to the cellar. Even on baking-day the whiff of cookies holds us only for a minute. We wait only to stuff our pockets. And at last the great day comes. The fresh wood is piled to the ceiling. It is a high mound and chaos, without form but certainly not void. For there are long pieces for bridges, flat pieces for theatre scenery, tall pieces for towers and grooves for marbles. It is a vast quarry for our pleasant use. You will please leave us in the twilight, sustained by doughnuts, burrowing in the pile, throwing out sticks to replenish our chest of blocks.

And therefore on this Christmas night, as I stand before the toy-shop in the whirling storm, the wind brings me the laughter of these far-off children. The snow of thirty winters is piled in my darkened memory, but I hear shrill voices across the night.

Sic Transit—

I DO not recall a feeling of greater triumph than on last Saturday when I walked off the eighteenth green of the Country Club with my opponent four down. I have the card before me now with its pleasant row of fives and sixes, and a four, *and a three.* Usually my card has mounted here and there to an eight or nine, or I have blown up altogether in a sandpit. Like Byron—but, oh, how differently!—I have wandered in the pathless wood. Like Ruth I have stood in tears amid the alien corn.

In those old days—only a week ago, but dim already (so soon does time wash the memory white)—in those old days, if I were asked to make up a foursome, some green inferior fellow, a novice who used his sister's clubs, was paired against me; or I was insulted with two strokes a hole, with three on the long hole past the woods. But now I shall ascend to faster company. It was my elbow. I now square it and cock it forward a bit. And I am cured. Keep your head down, Fritzie Boy, I say. Mind your elbow—I say it aloud—and I have no trouble.

There is a creek across the course. Like a thread in the woof it cuts the web of nearly every green. It is a black strand that puts trouble in the pattern, an evil thread from Clotho's ancient loom. Up at the sixth hole this creek is merely a dirty rivulet and I can

get out of the damned thing—one must write, they
say, as one talks and not go on stilts—I can get out
with a niblick by splashing myself a bit. But even
here, in its tender youth, as it were, the rivulet makes
all the mischief that it can. Gargantua with his
nurses was not so great a rogue. It crawls back and
forth three times before the tee with a kind of jeering
tongue stuck out. It seems foredoomed from the
cradle to a villainous course. Farther down, at the
seventeenth and second holes, which are near together,
it cuts a deeper chasm. The bank is shale and steep.
As I drive I feel like a black sinner on the nearer
shore of Styx, gazing upon the sunny fields of Para-
dise beyond. I put my caddy at the top of the slope,
where he sits with his apathetic eye upon the sullen,
predestined pool.

But since last Saturday all is different. I sailed
across on every drive, on every approach. The depths
beckoned but I heeded not. And, when I walked
across the bridge, I snapped my fingers in contempt,
as at a dog that snarls safely on a leash.

I play best with a niblick. It is not entirely that I
use it most. (Any day you can hear me bawling to
my caddy to fetch it behind a bunker or beyond a
fence.) Rather, the surface of the blade turns up at
a reassuring, hopeful angle. Its shining eye seems
cast at heaven in a prayer. I have had spells, also, of
fondness for my mashie. It is fluted for a back-spin.
Except for the click and flight of a prosperous drive I
know nothing of prettier symmetry than an accurate

approach. But my brassie I consider a reckless creature. It has bad direction. It treads not in the
narrow path. I have driven. Good! For once I am
clear of the woods. That white speck on the fairway
is my ball. But shall my ambition o'erleap itself?
Shall I select my brassie and tempt twice the gods of
chance? No! I'll use my mashie. I'll creep up to
the hole on hands and knees and be safe from trap
and ditch.

Has anyone spent more time than I among the
blackberry bushes along the railroad tracks on the
eleventh? It is no grossness of appetite. My niblick
grows hot with its exertions.

Once our course was not beset with sandpits. In
those bright days woods and gulley were enough.
Once clear of the initial obstruction I could roll up
unimpeded to the green. I practiced a bouncing
stroke with my putter that offered security at twenty
yards. But now these approaches are guarded by
traps. The greens are balanced on little mountains
with sharp ditches all about. I hoist up from one to
fall into another. "What a word, my son, has passed
the barrier of your teeth!" said Athene once to Odys-
seus. Is the game so ancient? Were there sandpits,
also, on the hills of stony Ithaca? Or in Ortygia, sea-
girt? Was the dear wanderer off his game and fallen
to profanity? The white-armed nymph Calypso must
have stuffed her ears.

But now my troubles are behind me. I have cured
my elbow of its fault. I keep my head down. My

very clubs have taken on a different look since Saturday. I used to remark their nicks against the stones.
A bit of green upon the heel of my driver showed how
it was that I went sidewise to the woods. In those
days I carried the bag spitefully to the shower.
Could I leave it, I pondered, as a foundling in an
empty locker? Or should I strangle it? But now all
is changed. My clubs are servants to my will, kindly,
obedient creatures that wait upon my nod. Even my
brassie knows me for its master. And the country
seems fairer. The valleys smile at me. The creek is
friendly to my drive. The tall hills skip and clap their
hands at my approach. My game needs only thought
and care. My fives will become fours, my sixes slip
down to fives. And here and there I shall have a
three.

Except for a row of books my mantelpiece is bare.
Who knows? Some day I may sweep off a musty row
of history and set up a silver cup.

Later—Saturday again. I have just been around
in 123. Horrible! I was in the woods and in the
blackberry bushes, and in the creek seven times. My
envious brassie! My well-belovèd mashie! Oh, vile
conspiracy! Ambition's debt is paid. 123! Now—
now it's my shoulder.

The Posture of Authors.

THERE is something rather pleasantly sug-
gestive in the fashion employed by many of
the older writers of inscribing their books from
their chambers or lodging. It gives them at once
locality and circumstance. It brings them to our
common earth and understanding. Thomas Fuller,
for example, having finished his Church History of
Britain, addressed his reader in a preface from his
chambers in Sion College. "May God alone have the
glory," he writes, "and the ingenuous reader the bene-
fit, of my endeavors! which is the hearty desire of Thy
servant in Jesus Christ, Thomas Fuller."

One pictures a room in the Tudor style, with oak
wainscot, tall mullioned windows and leaded glass, a
deep fireplace and black beams above. Outside,

perhaps, is the green quadrangle of the college, cloistered within ancient buildings, with gay wall-flowers against the sober stones. Bells answer from tower to belfry in agreeable dispute upon the hour. They were cast in a quieter time and refuse to bicker on a paltry minute. The sunlight is soft and yellow with old age. Such a dedication from such a place might turn the most careless reader into scholarship. In the seat of its leaded windows even the quirk of a Latin sentence might find a meaning. Here would be a room in which to meditate on the worthies of old England, or to read a chronicle of forgotten kings, queens, and protesting lovers who have faded into night.

Here we see Thomas Fuller dip his quill and make a start. "I have sometimes solitarily pleased myself," he begins, and he gazes into the dark shadows of the room, seeing, as it were, the pleasant spectres of the past. Bishops of Britain, long dead, in stole and mitre, forgetful of their solemn office, dance in the firelight on his walls. Popes move in dim review across his studies and shake a ghostly finger at his heresy. The past is not a prude. To her lover she reveals her beauty. And the scholar's lamp is her marriage torch.

Nor need it entirely cool our interest to learn that Sion College did not slope thus in country fashion to the peaceful waters of the Cam, with its fringe of trees and sunny meadow; did not possess even a gothic tower and cloister. It was built on the site of an ancient priory, Elsing Spital, with almshouses attached, a Jesuit library and a college for the clergy. It was right in London, down near the Roman wall, in the heart of the tangled traffic, and street cries kept breaking in—muffins, perhaps, and hot spiced ginger-bread and broken glass. I hope, at least, that the good gentleman's rooms were up above, somewhat out of the clatter, where muffins had lost their shrillness. Gingerbread, when distance has reduced it to a pleas-ant tune, is not inclined to rouse a scholar from his meditation. And even broken glass is blunted on a journey to a garret. I hope that the old gentleman climbed three flights or more and that a range of chimney-pots was his outlook and speculation.

It seems as if a rather richer flavor were given to a book by knowing the circumstance of its composition. Not only would we know the complexion of a man, whether he "be a black or a fair man," as Addison suggests, "of a mild or choleric disposition, married or a bachelor," but also in what posture he works and what objects meet his eye when he squares his elbows and dips his pen. We are concerned whether sun-light falls upon his papers or whether he writes in shadow. Also, if an author's desk stands at a window, we are curious whether it looks on a street, or on a garden, or whether it squints blindly against a wall. A view across distant hills surely sweetens the imagi-nation, whereas the clatter of the city gives a shrewder twist to fancy.

And household matters are of proper concern. We

would like to be informed whether an author works in
the swirl of the common sitting-room. If he writes
within earshot of the kitchen, we should know it.
There has been debate whether a steam radiator chills
a poet as against an open fire, and whether a plot
keeps up its giddy pace upon a sweeping day. Histories have balked before a household interruption.
Novels have been checked by the rattle of a careless
broom. A smoky chimney has choked the sturdiest
invention.

If a plot goes slack perhaps it is a bursted pipe.
An incessant grocer's boy, unanswered on the back
porch, has often foiled the wicked Earl in his attempts
against the beautiful Pomona. Little did you think,
my dear madam, as you read your latest novel, that
on the very instant when the heroine, Mrs. Elmira
Jones, deserted her babies to follow her conscience
and become a movie actress—that on that very instant when she slammed the street door, the plumber
(the author's plumber) came in to test the radiator.
Mrs. Jones nearly took her death on the steps as she
waited for the plot to deal with her. Even a Marquis,
now and then, one of the older sort in wig and ruffles,
has been left—when the author's ashes have needed
attention—on his knees before the Lady Emily,
begging her to name the happy day.

Was it not Coleridge's cow that calved while he was
writing "Kubla Khan"? In burst the housemaid with
the joyful news. And that man from Porlock—men-
tioned in his letters—who came on business? Did he

not despoil the morning of its poetry? Did Wordsworth's pigs—surely he owned pigs—never get into
his neighbor's garden and need quick attention?
Martin Luther threw his inkpot, supposedly, at the
devil. Is it not more likely that it was at Annie, who
came to dust? Thackeray is said to have written
largely at his club, the Garrick or the Athenæum.
There was a general stir of feet and voices, but it was
foreign and did not plague him. A tinkle of glasses
in the distance, he confessed, was soothing, like a
waterfall.

Steele makes no complaint against his wife Prue,
but he seems to have written chiefly in taverns. In
the very first paper of the *Tatler* he gratifies our
natural curiosity by naming the several coffee-houses
where he intends to compose his thoughts. "Foreign
and domestic news," he says, "you will have from
Saint James's Coffee-House." Learning will proceed
from the Grecian. But "all accounts of gallantry,
pleasure and entertainment shall be under the article
of White's Chocolate-House." In the month of September, 1705, he continues, a gentleman "was washing
his teeth at a tavern window in Pall Mall, when a fine
equipage passed by, and in it, a young lady who
looked up at him; away goes the coach—" Away goes
the beauty, with an alluring smile—rather an am-
biguous smile, I'm afraid—across her silken shoulder.
But for the continuation of this pleasant scandal (you
may be sure that the pretty fellow was quite distracted

from his teeth) one must turn up the yellow pages of
the *Tatler*.

We may suppose that Steele called for pens and
paper and a sandbox, and took a table in one of
White's forward windows. He wished no garden
view or brick wall against the window. We may even
go so far as to assume that something in the way of
punch, or canary, or negus *luke, my dear,* was handy
at his elbow. His paragraphs are punctuated by the
gay procession of the street. Here goes a great dandy
in red heels, with lace at his beard and wrists. Here
is a scarlet captain who has served with Marlborough
and has taken a whole regiment of Frenchmen by the
nose. Here is the Lady Belinda in her chariot, who is
the pledge of all the wits and poets. That little pink
ear of hers has been rhymed in a hundred sonnets—
ear and tear and fear and near and dear. The King
has been toasted from her slipper. The pretty creature has been sitting at ombre for most of the night,
but now at four of the afternoon she takes the morning
air with her lap dog. That great hat and feather will
slay another dozen hearts between shop and shop. She
is attended by a female dragon, but contrives by accident to show an inch or so of charming stocking at
the curb. Steele, at his window, I'm afraid, forgets
for the moment his darling Prue and his promise to
be home.

There is something rather pleasant in knowing
where these old authors, who are now almost forgotten, wrote their books. Richardson wrote "Cla-

rissa" at Parson's Green. That ought not to interest us very much, for nobody reads "Clarissa" now. But we can picture the fat little printer reading his daily batch of tender letters from young ladies, begging him to reform the wicked Lovelace and turn the novel to a happy end. For it was issued in parts and so, of course, there was no opportunity for young ladies, however impatient, to thumb the back pages for the plot.

Richardson wrote "Pamela" at a house called the Grange, then in the open country just out of London. There was a garden at the back, and a grotto—one of the grottoes that had been the fashion for prosperous literary gentlemen since Pope had built himself one at Twickenham. Here, it is said, Richardson used to read his story, day by day, as it was freshly composed, to a circle of his lady admirers. Hugh Thompson has drawn the picture in delightful silhouette. The ladies listen in suspense—perhaps the wicked Master is just taking Pamela on his knee—their hands are raised in protest. La! The Monster! Their noses are pitched up to a high excitement. One old lady hangs her head and blushes at the outrage. Or does she cock her ear to hear the better?

Richardson had a kind of rocking-horse in his study and he took his exercise so between chapters. We may imagine him galloping furiously on the hearth-rug, then, quite refreshed, after four or five dishes of tea, hiding his villain once more under Pamela's bed. Did it never occur to that young lady to lift the valance? Half a dozen times at least he has come popping out after she has loosed her stays, once even when she has got her stockings off. Perhaps this is the dangerous moment when the old lady in the silhouette hung her head and blushed. If Pamela had gone rummaging vigorously with a poker beneath her bed she could have cooled her lover.

Goldsmith wrote his books, for the most part, in lodgings. We find him starving with the beggars in Axe Lane, advancing to Green Arbour Court—sending down to the cook-shop for a tart to make his supper—living in the Temple, as his fortunes mended. Was it not at his window in the Temple that he wrote part of his "Animated Nature"? His first chapter— four pages—is called a sketch of the universe. In four pages he cleared the beginning up to Adam. Could anything be simpler or easier? The clever fellow, no doubt, could have made the universe— actually made it out of chaos—stars and moon and fishes in the sea—in less than the allotted six days and not needed a rest upon the seventh. He could have gone, instead, in plum-colored coat—"in full fig"—to Vauxhall for a frolic. Goldsmith had nothing in particular outside of his window to look at but the stone flagging, a pump and a solitary tree. Of the whole green earth this was the only living thing. For a brief season a bird or two lodged there, and you may be sure that Goldsmith put the remnant of his crumbs upon the window casement. Perhaps it was here that he sent down to the cook-shop for a tart, and he and the birds made a common banquet across the glass.

Poets, depending on their circumstance, are supposed to write either in garrets or in gardens. Browning, it is true, lived at Casa Guidi, which was "yellow with sunshine from morning to evening," and here and there a prosperous Byron has a Persian carpet and mahogany desk. But, for the most part, we put our poets in garrets, as a cheap place that has the additional advantage of being nearest to the moon. From these high windows sonnets are thrown, on a windy night. Rhymes and fancies are roused by gazing on the stars. The rumble of the lower city is potent to start a metaphor. "These fringes of lamplight," it is written, "struggling up through smoke and thousandfold exhalation, some fathoms into the ancient reign of Night, what thinks Boötes of them, as he leads his Hunting-dogs over the Zenith in their leash of sidereal fire? That stifled hum of Midnight, when Traffic has lain down to rest. . . ."

Here, under a sloping roof, the poet sits, blowing at his fingers. Hogarth has drawn him—the *Distressed Poet*—cold and lean and shabby. That famous picture might have been copied from the life of any of a hundred creatures of "The Dunciad," and, with a change of costume, it might serve our time as well. The poor fellow sits at a broken table in the dormer. About him lie his scattered sheets. His wife mends his breeches. Outside the door stands a woman with the unpaid milk-score. There is not a penny in the place—and for food only half a loaf and something brewing in a kettle. You may remember that when Johnson was a young poet, just come to London, he lived with Mr. Cave in St. John's Gate. When there were visitors he ate his supper behind a screen because he was too shabby to show himself. I wonder what definition he gave the poet in his dictionary. If he wrote in his own experience, he put him down as a poor devil who was always hungry. But Chatterton actually died of starvation in a garret, and those other hundred poets of his time and ours got down to the bone and took to coughing. Perhaps we shall change our minds about that sonnet which we tossed lightly to the moon. The wind thrusts a cold finger through chink and rag. The stars travel on such lonely journeys. The jest loses its relish. Perhaps those merry verses to the Christmas—the sleigh bells and the roasted goose—perhaps those verses turn bitter when written on an empty stomach.

But do poets ever write in gardens? Swift, who was by way of being a poet, built himself a garden-seat at Moor Park when he served Sir William Temple, but I don't know that he wrote poetry there. Rather, it was a place for reading. Pope in his prosperous days wrote at Twickenham, with the sound of his artificial waterfall in his ears, and he walked to take the air in his grotto along the Thames. But do poets really wander beneath the moon to think their verses? Do they compose "on summer eve by haunted stream"? I doubt whether Gray conceived his Elegy

in an actual graveyard. I smell oil. One need
not see the thing described upon the very moment.
Shelley wrote of mountains—the awful range of Caucasus—but his eye at the time looked on sunny Italy.
Ibsen wrote of the north when living in the south.
When Bunyan wrote of the Delectable Mountains he
was snug inside a jail. Shakespeare, doubtless, saw
the giddy cliffs of Dover, the Rialto, the Scottish
heath, from the vantage of a London lodging.

Where did Andrew Marvell stand or sit or walk
when he wrote about gardens? Wordsworth is said to
have strolled up and down a gravel path with his eyes
on the ground. I wonder whether the gardener ever
broke in—if he had a gardener—to complain about
the drouth or how the dandelions were getting the
better of him. Or perhaps the lawn-mower squeaked
—if he had a lawn-mower—and threw him off. But
wasn't it Wordsworth who woke up four times in one
night and called to his wife for pens and paper lest an
idea escape him? Surely he didn't take to the garden
at that time of night in his pajamas with an inkpot.
But did Wordsworth have a wife? How one forgets!
Coleridge told Hazlitt that he liked to compose "walking over uneven ground, or breaking through the
straggling branches of a copse-wood." But then, you
recall that a calf broke into "Kubla Khan." On that
particular day, at least, he was snug in his study.

No, I think that poets may like to sit in gardens
and smoke their pipes and poke idly with their sticks,
but when it comes actually to composing they would

rather go inside. For even a little breeze scatters
their papers. No poet wishes to spend his precious
morning chasing a frisky sonnet across the lawn.
Even a heavy epic, if lifted by a sudden squall, chal-
lenges the swiftest foot. He puts his stick on one pile
and his pipe on another and he holds down loose sheets
with his thumb. But it is awkward business, and it
checks the mind in its loftier flight.

Nor do poets care to suck their pencils too long
where someone may see them—perhaps Annie at the
window rolling her pie-crust. And they can't kick
off their shoes outdoors in the hot agony of composition. And also, which caps the argument, a garden
is undeniably a sleepy place. The bees drone to a
sleepy tune. The breeze practices a lullaby. Even
the sunlight is in the common conspiracy. At the
very moment when the poet is considering Little Miss
Muffet and how she sat on a tuffet—doubtless in a
garden, for there were spiders—even at the very
moment when she sits unsuspectingly at her curds and
whey, down goes the poet's head and he is fast asleep.
Sleepiness is the plague of authors. You may remember that when Christian—who, doubtless, was an
author in his odd moments—came to the garden and
the Arbour on the Hill Difficulty, "he pulled his Roll
out of his bosom and read therein to his comfort. . . .
Thus pleasing himself awhile, he at last fell into a
slumber." I have no doubt—other theories to the contrary—that "Kubla Khan" broke off suddenly because
Coleridge dropped off to sleep. A cup of black coffee

might have extended the poem to another stanza. Mince pie would have stretched it to a volume. Is not Shakespeare allowed his forty winks? Has it not been written that even the worthy Homer nods?

"A pleasing land of drowsyhed it was:
  Of dreams that wave before the half-shut eye;
  And of gay castles in the clouds that pass,
  For ever flushing round a summer sky."

No, if one has a bit of writing to put out of the way, it is best to stay indoors. Choose an uncomfortable, straight-backed chair. Toss the sheets into a careless litter. And if someone will pay the milk-score and keep the window mended, a garret is not a bad place in which to write.

Novelists—unless they have need of history—can write anywhere, I suppose, at home or on a journey. In the burst of their hot imagination a knee is a desk. I have no doubt that Mr. Hugh Walpole, touring in this country, contrives to write a bit even in a Pullman. The ingenious Mr. Oppenheim surely dashes off a plot on the margin of the menu-card between meat and salad. We know that "Pickwick Papers" was written partly in hackney coaches while Dickens was jolting about the town.

An essayist, on the other hand, needs a desk and a library near at hand. Because an essay is a kind of back-stove cookery. A novel needs a hot fire, so to speak. A dozen chapters bubble in their turn above the reddest coals, while an essay simmers over a little flame. Pieces of this and that, an odd carrot, as it were, a left potato, a pithy bone, discarded trifles, are tossed in from time to time to enrich the composition. Raw paragraphs, when they have stewed all night, at last become tender to the fork. An essay, therefore, cannot be written hurriedly on the knee. Essayists, as a rule, chew their pencils. Their desks are large and are always in disorder. There is a stack of books on the clock shelf. Others are pushed under the bed. Matches, pencils and bits of paper mark a hundred references. When an essayist goes out from his lodging he wears the kind of overcoat that holds a book in every pocket. His sagging pockets proclaim him. He is a bulging person, so stuffed, even in his dress, with the ideas of others that his own leanness is concealed. An essayist keeps a notebook, and he thumbs it for forgotten thoughts. Nobody is safe from him, for he steals from everyone he meets.

An essayist is not a mighty traveler. He does not run to grapple with a roaring lion. He desires neither typhoon nor tempest. He is content in his harbor to listen to the storm upon the rocks, if now and then, by a lucky chance, he can shelter someone from the wreck. His hands are not red with revolt against the world. He has glanced upon the thoughts of many men; and as opposite philosophies point upon the truth, he is modest with his own and tolerant toward the opinion of others. He looks at the stars and, knowing in what a dim immensity we travel, he writes of little things beyond dispute. There are enough to weep upon the shadows, he, like a dial, marks the light. The small clatter of the city beneath his window, the cry of peddlers, children chalking their games upon the pavement, laundry dancing on the roofs and smoke in the winter's wind—these are the things he weaves into the fabric of his thoughts. Or sheep upon the hillside—if his window is so lucky—or a sunny meadow, is a profitable speculation. And so, while the novelist is struggling up a dizzy mountain, straining through the tempest to see the kingdoms of the world, behold the essayist snug at home, content with little sights. He is a kind of poet—a poet whose wings are clipped. He flaps to no great heights and sees neither the devil, the seven oceans nor the twelve apostles. He paints old thoughts in shiny varnish and, as he is able, he mends small habits here and there. And therefore, as essayists stay at home, they are precise—almost amorous—in the posture and outlook of their writing. Leigh Hunt wished a great library next his study. "But for the study itself," he writes, "give me a small snug place, almost entirely walled with books. There should be only one window in it looking upon trees." How the precious fellow scorns the mountains and the ocean! He has no love, it seems, for typhoons and roaring lions. "I entrench myself in my books," he continues, "equally against sorrow and the weather. If the wind comes through a passage, I look about to see how I can fence it off by a better disposition of my movables." And by movables he means his books. These were his screen against cold and trouble. But

Leigh Hunt had been in prison for his political beliefs.
He had grappled with his lion.   So perhaps, after all,
my argument fails.

Mr. Edmund Gosse had a different method to the
same purpose.   He "was so anxious to fly all outward
noise" that he desired a library apart from the house.
Maybe he had had some experience with Annie and
her clattering broomstick.   "In my sleep," he writes,
" 'Where dreams are multitude,' I sometimes fancy
that one day I shall have a library in a garden.   The
phrase seems to contain the whole felicity of man. . . .
It sounds like having a castle in Spain, or a sheep-
walk in Arcadia."

Montaigne's study was a tower, walled all about
with books.   At his table in the midst he was the
general focus of their wisdom.   Hazlitt wrote much at
an inn at Winterslow, with Salisbury Plain around
the corner of his view.   Now and then, let us hope,
when the London coach was due, he received in his
nostrils a savory smell from the kitchen stove.   I
taste pepper, sometimes, and sharp sauces in his
writing.   Stevenson, except for ill-health and a love
of the South Seas (here was the novelist showing
himself), would have preferred a windy perch over-
looking Edinburgh.

It does seem as if a rather richer flavor were given
to a book by knowing the circumstance of its composition.   Consequently, readers, as they grow older,
turn more and more to biography.   It is chiefly not the
biographies that deal with great crises and events, but

rather the biographies that are concerned with small circumstance and agreeable gossip, that attract them most. The life of Gladstone, with its hard facts of British policy, is all very well; but Mr. Lucas's life of Lamb is better. Who would willingly neglect the record of a Thursday night at Inner Temple Lane? In these pages Talfourd, Procter, Hazlitt and Hunt have written their memories of these gatherings. It was to his partner at whist, as he was dealing, that Lamb once said, "If dirt was trumps, what hands you would hold!" Nights of wit and friendly banter! Who would not crowd his ears with gossip of that mirthful company?—George Dyer, who forgot his boots until half way home (the dear fellow grew forgetful as the smoking jug went round)—Charles Lamb feeling the stranger's bumps. Let the Empire totter! Let Napoleon fall! Africa shall be parceled as it may. Here will we sit until the cups are empty.

Lately, in a bookshop at the foot of Cornhill, I fell in with an old scholar who told me that it was his practice to recommend four books, which, taken end on end, furnished the general history of English letters from the Restoration to a time within our own memory. These books were "Pepys' Diary," "Boswell's Johnson," the "Diary and Letters of Madame d'Arblay" and the "Diary of Crabb Robinson."

Beginning almost with the days of Cromwell here is a chain of pleasant gossip across the space of more than two hundred years. Perhaps, at the first, there were old fellows still alive who could remember

Shakespeare—who still sat in chimney corners and babbled through their toothless gums of Blackfriars and the Globe.   And at the end we find a reference to President Lincoln and the freeing of the slaves.

Here are a hundred authors—perhaps a thousand—tucking up their cuffs, looking out from their familiar windows, scribbling their large or trivial masterpieces.

After-Dinner Pleasantries.

THERE is a shop below Fourteenth Street, somewhat remote from fashion, that sells nothing but tricks for amateur and parlor use. It is a region of cobblers, tailors and small grocers. Upstairs, locksmiths and buttonhole cutters look through dusty windows on the L, which, under some dim influence of the moon, tosses past the buildings here its human tide, up and down, night and morning. The Trick Shop flatters itself on its signboard that it carries the largest line of its peculiar trickery on the western hemisphere—hinting modestly that Baluchistan, perhaps, or Mesopotamia (where magic might be supposed to flourish) may have an equal stock. The shop does not proclaim its greatness to the casual glance. Its enormity of fraud offers no hint to the unsuspecting curb. There must be caverns and cellars at the rear—a wealth of baffling sham un-rumored to the street, shelves sagging with agreeable deception, huge bales of sleight-of-hand and musty barrels of old magic.

But to the street the shop reveals no more than a small show-window, of a kind in which licorice-sticks and all-day-suckers might feel at home. It is a window at which children might stop on their way from school and meditate their choice, fumbling in their pockets for their wealth.

I have stood at this window for ten minutes to-gether. There are cards for fortune tellers and manuals of astrology, decks with five aces and marked backs, and trick hats and boxes with false bottoms. There are iron cigars to be offered to a friend, and bleeding fingers, and a device that makes a noise like blowing the nose, "only much louder." Books of magic are displayed, and conjurers' outfits—shell games and disappearing rabbits. There is a line of dribble-glasses—a humorous contrivance with little holes under the brim for spilling water down the front of an unwary guest. This, it is asserted, breaks the social ice and makes a timid stranger feel at home. And there are puzzle pictures, beards for villains and comic masks—Satan himself, and other painted faces for Hallowe'en.

Some persons, of course, can perform their parlor tricks without this machinery and appliance. I know a gifted fellow who can put on the expression of an idiot. Or he wrinkles his face into the semblance of eighty years, shakes with palsy and asks his tired wife if she will love him when he's old. Again he puts a coffee cup under the shoulder of his coat and plays the humpback. On a special occasion he mounts a table—or two kitchen chairs become his stage—and recites Richard and the winter of his discontent. He needs only a pillow to smother Desdemona. And then he opens an imaginary bottle—the popping of the cork, the fizzing, the gurgle when it pours. Sometimes he is a squealing pig caught under a fence, and sometimes two steamboats signaling with their whistles in a fog.

I know a young woman—of the newer sort—who appears to swallow a lighted cigarette, with smoke coming from her ears. This was once a man's trick, but the progress of the weaker sex has shifted it. On request, she is a nervous lady with a fear of monkeys, taking five children to the circus. She is Camille on her deathbed. I know a man, too, who can give the Rebel yell and stick a needle, full length, into his leg. The pulpy part above his knee seems to make an excellent pincushion. And then there is the old locomotive starting on a slippery grade (for beginners in entertainment), the hand-organ man and his infested monkey (a duet), the chicken that is chased around the barnyard, Hamlet with the broken pallet (this is side-splitting in any company) and Moriarty on the telephone. I suppose our best vaudeville performers were once amateurs themselves around the parlor lamp.

And there is Jones, too, who plays the piano. Jones, when he is asked, sits at the keyboard and fingers little runs and chords. He seems to be thinking which of a hundred pieces he will play. "What will you have?" he asks. And a fat man wants "William Tell," and a lady with a powdered nose asks for "Bubbles." But Jones ignores both and says, "Here's a little thing of Schumann. It's a charming bit." On the other hand, when Brown is asked to sing, it is generally too soon after dinner. Brown, evidently, takes his food through his windpipe, and it is, so to speak, a one-way street. He can hardly permit the ascending "Siegfried" to squeeze past the cheese and crackers that still block the crowded passage.

There is not a college dinner without the mockery of an eccentric professor. A wag will catch the pointing of his finger, his favorite phrase. Is there a lawyers' dinner without its imitation of Harry Lauder? Isn't there always someone who wants to sing "It's Nice to Get Up in the Mornin'," and trot up and down with twinkling legs? Plumbers on their lodge nights, I am told, have their very own Charlie Chaplin. And I suppose that the soda clerks' union—the dear creatures with their gum—has its local Mary Pickford, ready with a scene from *Pollyanna*. What jolly dinners dentists must have, telling one another in dialect how old Mrs. Finnigan had her molars out!

Forceps and burrs are their unwearied jest across the years. When they are together and the doors are closed, how they must frolic with our weakness!

And undertakers! Even they, I am informed, throw off their solemn countenance when they gather in convention. Their carnation and mournful smile are gone—that sober gesture that waves the chilly relations to the sitting-room. But I wonder whether their dismal shop doesn't cling always just a bit to their mirth and songs. That poor duffer in the poem who asked to be laid low, wrapped in his tarpaulin jacket—surely, undertakers never sing of him. They must look at him with disfavor for his cheap proposal. He should have roused for a moment at the end, with a request for black broadcloth and silver handles.

I once sat with an undertaker at a tragedy. He was of a lively sympathy in the earlier parts and seemed hopeful that the hero would come through alive. But in the fifth act, when the clanking army was defeated in the wings and Brutus had fallen on his sword, then, unmistakably his thoughts turned to the peculiar viewpoint of his profession. In fancy he sat already in the back parlor with the grieving Mrs. Brutus, arranging for the music.

To undertakers, Cæsar is always dead and turned to clay. Falstaff is just a fat old gentleman who drank too much sack, a' babbled of green fields and then needed professional attention. Perhaps at the very pitch of their meetings when the merry glasses have been three times filled, they pledge one another in what they are pleased to call the embalmers' fluid. This jest grows rosier with the years. For these many centuries at their banquets they have sung that it was a cough that carried him off, that it was a coffin—Now then, gentlemen! All together for the chorus!—that it was a coffin they carried him off in.

I dined lately with a man who could look like a weasel. When this was applauded, he made a face like the Dude of *Palmer Cox's Brownies*. Even Susan, the waitress, who knows her place and takes a jest soberly, broke down at the pantry door. We could hear her dishes rattling in convulsions in the sink. And then our host played the insect with his fingers on the tablecloth, smelling a spot of careless gravy from the roast with his long thin middle finger. He caught the habit that insects have of waving their forward legs.

I still recall an uncle who could wiggle his ears. He did it every Christmas and Thanksgiving Day. It was as much a part of the regular program as the turkey and the cranberries. It was a feature of his engaging foolery to pretend that the wiggle was produced by rubbing the stomach, and a circle of us youngsters sat around him, rubbing our expectant stomachs, waiting for the miracle. A cousin brought a guitar and played the "Spanish Fandango" while we sat around the fire, sleepy after dinner. And there was a maiden aunt with thin blue fingers, who played waltzes while we danced, and she nodded and slept to the drowsy sound of her own music.

Of my own after-dinner pleasantries I am modest. I have only one trick. Two. I can recite the fur-bearing animals of North America—the bison, the bear, the wolf, the seal, and sixteen others—and I can go downstairs behind the couch for the cider. This last requires little skill. As the books of magic say, it is an easy and baffling trick. With every step you crook your legs a little more, until finally you are on your knees, hunched together, and your head has disappeared from view. You reverse the business coming up, with tray and glasses.

But these are my only tricks. There is a Brahms waltz that I once had hopes of, but it has a hard run on the second page. I can never get my thumb under in time to make connections. My best voice, too, covers only five notes. You cannot do much for the neighbors with that cramped kind of range. "A Tailor There Sat on His Window Ledge" is one of the few tunes that fall inside my poverty. He calls to his wife, you may remember, to bring him his old cross-bow, and there is a great Zum! Zum! up and down in the bass until ready, before the chorus starts. On a foggy morning I have quite a formidable voice for those Zums. But after-dinner pleasantries are only good at night and then my bass is thin. "A Sailor's Life, Yo, Ho!" is a very good tune but it goes up to D, and I can sing it only when I am reck-less of circumstance, or when I am taking ashes from the furnace. I know a lady who sings only at her sewing-machine. She finds a stirring accompaniment

in the whirling of the wheel. Others sing best in tiled
bathrooms. Sitting in warm and soapy water their
voices swell to Caruso's. Laundresses, I have noticed,
are in lustiest voice at their tubs, where their arms
keep a vigorous rhythm on the scrubbing-board. But
I choose ashes. I am little short of a Valkyr, despite
my sex, when I rattle the furnace grate.

With hymns I can make quite a showing in church
if the bass part keeps to a couple of notes. I pound
along melodiously on some convenient low note and
slide up now and then, by a happy instinct, when the
tune seems to require it. The dear little lady, who
sits in front of me, turns what I am pleased to think
is an appreciative ear, and now and then, for my support, she throws in a pretty treble. But I have no
tolerance with a bass part that undertakes a flourish
and climbs up behind the tenor. This is mere egotism
and a desire to shine. "Art thou there, true-penny?
You hear this fellow in the cellarage?" That is the
proper bass.

Dear me! Now that I recall it, we have guests—
guests tonight for dinner. Will I be asked to sing?
Am I in voice? I tum-a-lum a little, up and down, for
experiment. The roar of the subway drowns this
from my neighbors, but by holding my hand over my
mouth I can hear it. Is my low F in order? No—
undeniably, it is not. Thin. And squeaky. The
Zums would never do. And that fast run in Brahms?
Can I slip through it? Or will my thumb, as usual,
catch and stall? Have my guests seen me go down-

stairs behind the couch for the cider? Have they heard the fur-bearing animals—the bison, the bear, the wolf, the seal, the beaver, the otter, the fox and raccoon?

Perhaps—perhaps it will be better to stop at the Trick Shop and buy a dribble-glass and a long black beard to amuse my guests.

Little Candles.

HIGH conceit of one's self and a sureness of one's opinion are based so insecurely in experience that one is perplexed how their slight structure stands. One marvels why these emphatic builders trust again their glittering towers. Surely anyone who looks into himself and sees its void or malformation ought by rights to shrink from adulation of self, and his own opinion should appear to him merely as one candle among a thousand.

And yet this conceit of self outlasts innumerable failures, and any new pinnacle that is set up, neglecting the broken rubble on the ground and all the wreckage at the base, boasts again of its sure communion with the stars. A man, let us say, has gone headlong from one formula of belief into another. In each, for a time, he burns with a hot conviction. Then his faith cools. His god no longer nods. But just when you think that failure must have brought him modesty, again he amazes you with the golden prospect of a new adventure. He has climbed in his life a hundred hillocks, thinking each to be a mountain. He has journeyed on many paths, but always has fallen in a bog. Conceit is a thin bubble in the wind, it is an empty froth and breath, yet, hammered into ship-plates, it defies the U-boat.

On every sidewalk, also, we see some fine fellow, dressed and curled to his satisfaction, parading in the sun. An accident of wealth or birth has marked him from the crowd. He has decked his outer walls in gaudy color, but is bare within. He is a cypher, but golden circumstance, like a figure in the million column, gives him substance. Yet the void cries out on all matters in dispute with firm conviction.

But this cypher need not dress in purple. He is shabby, let us say, and pinched with poverty. Whose fault? Who knows? But does misfortune in itself give wisdom? He is poor. Therefore he decides that the world is sick with pestilence, and accordingly he proclaims himself a doctor. Or perhaps he sits at ease in middle circumstance. He judges that his is an open mind because he lets a harsh opinion blow upon his ignorance until it flames with hatred. He sets up to be a thinker, and he is resolved to shatter the foundations of a thousand years.

The outer darkness stretches to such a giddy distance! And these thousand candles of belief, flickering in the night, are so insufficient even in their aggre-

gate! Shall a candle wink at flaming Jupiter as an
equal? By what persuasion is one's own tiny wick,
shielded in the fingers from misadventure, the greatest
light?

Who is there who has read more than a single chapter in the book of life? Most of us have faltered
through scarcely a dozen paragraphs, yet we scribble
our sure opinion in the margin. We hear a trifling
pebble fall in a muddy pool, and we think that we have
listened to the pounding of the sea. We hold up our
little candle and we consider that its light dispels the
general night.

But it has happened once in a while that someone
really strikes a larger light and offers it to many
travelers for their safety. He holds his candle above
his head for the general comfort. And to it there rush
the multitude of those whose candles have been gutted.
They relight their wicks, and go their way with a song
and cry, to announce their brotherhood. If they see a
stranger off the path, they call to him to join their
band. And they draw him from the mire.

And sometimes this company respects the other
candles that survive the wind. They confess with
good temper that their glare, also, is sufficient; that
there is, indeed, more than one path across the night.
But sometimes in their intensity—in their sureness of
exclusive salvation—they fall to bickering. One band
of converts elbows another. There is a mutual lifting
of the nose in scorn, an amused contempt, or they come
to blows and all candles are extinguished. And some-

times, with candles out, they travel onward, still telling one another of their band how the darkness flees before them.

We live in a world of storm, of hatred, of blind conceit, of shrill and intolerant opinion. The past is worshiped. The past is scorned. Some wish only to kiss the great toe of old convention. Others shout that we must run bandaged in the dark, if we would prove our faith in God and man. It is the best of times, and the worst of times. It is the dawn. We grope toward midnight. Our fathers were saints in judgment. Our fathers were fools and rogues. Let's hold minutely to the past! Any change is sacrilege. Let's rip it up! Let's destroy it altogether!

We'll kill him and stamp on him: He's a Montague. We'll draw and quarter him: He's a Capulet. He's a radical: He must be hanged. A conservative: His head shall decorate our pike.

A plague on both your houses!

Panaceas are hawked among us, each with a magic to cure our ills. Universal suffrage is a leap to perfection. Tax reform will bring the golden age. With capital and interest smashed, we shall live in heaven. The soviet, the recall from office, the six-hour day, the demands of labor, mark the better path. The greater clamor of the crowd is the guide to wisdom. Men with black beards and ladies with cigarettes say that machine-guns and fire and death are pills that are potent for our good. We live in a welter of quarrel and disagreement. One pictures a mighty shelf with

bottles, and doctors running to and fro. The poor
world is on its back, opening its mouth to every spoon.
By the hubbub in the pantry—the yells and scuffling
at the sink—we know that drastic and contrary cures
are striving for the mastery.

There was a time when beacons burned on the hills
to be our guidance. The flames were fed and moulded
by the experience of the centuries. Men might differ
on the path—might even scramble up a dozen different
slopes—but the hill-top was beyond dispute.

But now the great fires smoulder. The Constitu-
tion, it is said,—pecked at since the first,—must now
be carted off and sold as junk. Art has torn down
its older standards. The colors of Titian are in the
dust. Poets no longer bend the knee to Shakespeare.

Conceit is a pilot who scorns the harbor lights—

Modesty was once a virtue. Patience, diligence,
thrift, humility, charity—who pays now a tribute to
them? Charity is only a sop, it seems, that is thrown
in fright to the swift wolves of revolution. Humility is now a weakness. Diligence is despised. Thrift
is the advice of cowards. Who now cares for the
lessons that experience and tested fact once taught?
Ignorance sits now in the highest seat and gives its
orders, and the clamor of the crowd is its high
authority.

And what has become of modesty? A maid once
was prodigal if she unmasked her beauty to the moon.
Morality? Let's all laugh together. It's a quaint old
word.

Tolerance is the last study in the school of wisdom. Lord! Lord! Tonight let my prayer be that I may know that my own opinion is but a candle in the wind!

A Visit to a Poet.

NOT long ago I accepted the invitation of a young poet to visit him at his lodging. As my life has fallen chiefly among merchants, lawyers and other practical folk, I went with much curiosity.

My poet, I must confess, is not entirely famous. His verses have appeared in several of the less known papers, and a judicious printer has even offered to gather them into a modest sheaf. There are, however, certain vile details of expense that hold up the project. The printer, although he confesses their merit, feels that the poet should bear the cost.

His verses are of the newer sort. When read aloud they sound pleasantly in the ear, but I sometimes miss the meaning. I once pronounced an intimate soul-study to be a jolly description of a rainy night. This was my stupidity. I could see a soul quite plainly when it was pointed out. It was like looking at the moon. You get what you look for—a man or a woman or a kind of map of Asia. In poetry of this sort I need a hint or two to start me right. But when my nose has been rubbed, so to speak, against the anise-bag, I am a very hound upon the scent.

The street where my friend lives is just north of Greenwich Village, and it still shows a remnant of more aristocratic days. Behind its shabby fronts are long drawing-rooms with tarnished glass chandeliers and frescoed ceilings and gaunt windows with inside blinds. Plaster cornices still gather the dust of years. There are heavy stairways with black walnut rails. Marble Lincolns still liberate the slaves in niches of the hallway. Bronze Ladies of the Lake await their tardy lovers. Diana runs with her hunting dogs upon the newel post. In these houses lived the heroines of sixty years ago, who shopped for crinoline and spent their mornings at Stewart's to match a Godey pattern. They drove of an afternoon with gay silk parasols to the Crystal Palace on Forty-second Street. In short, they were our despised Victorians. With our advancement we have made the world so much better since.

I pressed an electric button. Then, as the door clicked, I sprang against it. These patent catches throw me into a momentary panic. I feel like one of the foolish virgins with untrimmed lamp, just about to be caught outside—but perhaps I confuse the legend. Inside, there was a bare hallway, with a series of stairways rising in the gloom—round and round, like the frightful staircase of the Opium Eater. At the top of the stairs a black disk hung over the rail—probably a head.

"Hello," I said.

"Oh, it's you. Come up!" And the poet came down to meet me, with slippers slapping at the heels.

There was a villainous smell on the stairs. "Something burning?" I asked.

At first the poet didn't smell it. "Oh, *that* smell!" he said at last. "That's the embalmer."

"The embalmer?"

We were opposite a heavy door on the second floor. He pointed his thumb at it. "There's an embalmer's school inside."

"Dear me!" I said. "Has he any—anything to practice on?"

The poet pushed the door open a crack. It was very dark inside. It smelled like Ptolemy in his later days. Or perhaps I detected Polonius, found at last beneath the stairs.

"Bless me!" I asked, "What does he teach in his school?"

"Embalming, and all that sort of thing."

"It never occurred to me," I confessed, "that undertakers had to learn. I thought it came naturally. Ducks to water, you know. They look as if they could pick up a thing like embalming by instinct. I don't suppose you knew old Mr. Smith."

"No."

"He wore a white carnation on business afternoons."

We rounded a turn of the black walnut stair.

"There!" exclaimed the poet. "That is the office of the *Shriek.*"

I know the *Shriek.* It is one of the periodicals of the newer art that does not descend to the popular taste. It will not compromise its ideals. It prints pictures of men and women with hideous, distorted bodies. It is solving sex. Once in a while the police know what it is talking about, and then they rather stupidly keep it out of the mails for a month or so.

Now I had intended for some time to subscribe to the *Shriek,* because I wished to see my friend's verses as they appeared. In this way I could learn what the newer art was doing, and could brush out of my head the cobwebs of convention. Keats and Shelley have been thrown into the discard. We have come a long journey from the older poets.

"I would like to subscribe," I said.

The poet, of course, was pleased. He rapped at a door marked "Editor."

A young woman's head in a mob-cap came into view. She wore a green and purple smock, and a cigarette hung loosely from her mouth. She looked at me at first as if I were an old-fashioned poem or a bundle of modest drawings, but cheered when I told my errand. There was a cup of steaming soup on an alcohol burner, and half a loaf of bread. On a string across the window handkerchiefs and stockings were hung to dry. A desk was littered with papers.

I paid my money and was enrolled. I was given a current number of the *Shriek,* and was told not to miss a poem by Sillivitch.

"Sillivitch?" I asked.

"Sillivitch," the lady answered. "Our greatest poet —maybe the greatest of all time. Writes only for the *Shriek.* Wonderful! Realistic!"

"Snug little office," I said to the poet, when we were on the stairs. "She lives in there, too?"

"Oh, yes," he said. "Smart girl, that. Never compromises. Wants reality and all that sort of thing. You must read Sillivitch. Amazing! Doesn't seem to mean anything at first. But then you get it in a flash."

We had now come to the top of the building.

"There isn't much smell up here," I said.

"You don't mind the smell. You come to like it," he replied. "It's bracing."

At the top of the stairs, a hallway led to rooms both front and back. The ceiling of these rooms, low even in the middle, sloped to windows of half height in dormers. The poet waved his hand. "I have been living in the front room," he said, "but I am adding this room behind for a study."

We entered the study. A man was mopping up the floor. Evidently the room had not been lived in for years, for the dirt was caked to a half inch. A general wreckage of furniture—a chair, a table with marble top, a carved sideboard with walnut dingles, a wooden bed with massive headboard, a mattress and a broken pitcher—had been swept to the middle of the room. There was also a pile of old embalmer's journals, and a great carton that seemed to contain tubes of toothpaste.

"You see," said the poet, "I have been living in the other room. This used to be a storage—years ago, for the family that once lived here, and more recently for the embalmer."

"Storage!" I exclaimed. "You don't suppose that they kept any—?"

"No."

"Well," I said, "it's a snug little place."

I bent over and picked up one of the embalmer's journals. On the cover there was a picture of a little boy in a night-gown, saying his prayer to his mother. The prayer was printed underneath. "And, mama," it read, "have God make me a good boy, and when I grow up let me help papa in his business, and never use anything but *Twirpp's Old Reliable Embalming Fluid,* the kind that papa has always used, and grandpa before him."

Now, Charles Lamb, I recall, once confessed that he was moved to enthusiasm by an undertaker's advertisement. "Methinks," he writes, "I could be willing to die, in death to be so attended. The two rows all round close-drove best black japanned nails,—how feelingly do they invite, and almost irresistibly persuade us to come and be fastened down." But the journal did not stir me to this high emotion.

I crossed the room and stooped to look out of the dormer window—into a shallow yard where an abandoned tin bath-tub and other unprized valuables were kept. A shabby tree acknowledged that it had lost its way, but didn't know what to do about it. It had its elbow on the fence and seemed to be in thought. A wash-stand lay on its side, as if it snapped its fingers

forever at soap and towels. Beyond was a tall building, with long tables and rows of girls working.

One of the girls desisted for a moment from her
feathers with which she was making hats, and stuck
out her tongue at me in a coquettish way. I returned
her salute. She laughed and tossed her head and went
back to her feathers.

The young man who had been mopping up the floor
went out for fresh water.

"Who is that fellow?" I asked.

"He works downstairs."

"For the *Shriek?*"

"For the embalmer. He's an apprentice."

"I would like to meet him."

Presently I did meet him.

"What have you there?" I asked. He was folding
up a great canvas bag of curious pattern.

"It's when you are shipped away—to Texas or
somewhere. This is a little one. You'd need—" he
appraised me from head to foot—"you'd need a number ten."

He desisted from detail. He shifted to the story of
his life. Since he had been a child he had wished to
be an undertaker.

Now I had myself once known an undertaker, and
I had known his son. The son went to Munich to
study for Grand Opera. I crossed on the steamer
with him. He sang in the ship's concert, "Oh, That
We Two Were Maying." It was pitched for high
tenor, so he sang it an octave low, and was quite

gloomy about it. In the last verse he expressed a desire to lie at rest beneath the churchyard sod. The boat was rolling and I went out to get the air. And then I did not see him for several years. We met at a funeral. He wore a long black coat and a white carnation. He smiled at me with a gentle, mournful smile and waved me to a seat. He was Tristan no longer. Valhalla no more echoed to his voice. He had succeeded to his father's business.

Here the poet interposed. "The Countess came to see me yesterday."

"Mercy," I said, "what countess?"

"Oh, don't you know her work? She's a poet and she writes for the people downstairs. She's the Countess Sillivitch."

"Sillivitch!" I answered, "of course I know her. She is the greatest poet, maybe, of all time."

"No doubt about it," said the poet excitedly, "and there's a poem of hers in this number. She writes in italics when she wants you to yell it. And when she puts it in capitals, my God! you could hear her to the elevated. It's ripping stuff."

"Dear me," I said, "I should like to read it. Awfully. It must be funny."

"It isn't funny at all," the poet answered. "It isn't meant to be funny. Did you read her 'Burning Kiss'?"

"I'm sorry," I answered.

The poet sighed. "It's wonderfully realistic.

There's nothing old-fashioned about that poem. The Countess wears painted stockings."

"Bless me!" I cried.

"Stalks with flowers. She comes from Bulgaria, or Esthonia, or somewhere. Has a husband in a castle. Incompatible. He stifles her. Common. In business. Beer spigots. She is artistic. Wants to soar. And tragic. You remember my study of a soul?"

"The rainy night? Yes, I remember."

"Well, she's the one. She sat on the floor and told me her troubles."

"You don't suppose that I could meet her, do you?" I asked.

The poet looked at me with withering scorn. "You wouldn't like her," he said. "She's very modern. She says very startling things. You have to be in the modern spirit to follow her. And sympathetic. She doesn't want any marriage or government or things like that. Just truth and freedom. It's convention that clips our wings."

"Conventions are stupid things," I agreed.

"And the past isn't any good, either," the poet said. "The past is a chain upon us. It keeps us off the mountains."

"Exactly," I assented.

"That's what the Countess thinks. We must destroy the past. Everything. Customs. Art. Government. We must be ready for the coming of the dawn."

"Naturally," I said. "Candles trimmed, and all that sort of thing. You don't suppose that I could meet the Countess? Well, I'm sorry. What's the bit of red paper on the wall? Is it over a dirty spot?"

"It's to stir up my ideas. It's gay and when I look at it I think of something."

"And then I suppose that you look out of that window, against that brick wall and those windows opposite, and write poems—a sonnet to the girl who stuck out her tongue at me."

"Oh, yes."

"Hot in summer up here?"

"Yes."

"And cold in winter?"

"Yes."

"And I suppose that you get some ideas out of that old tin bath-tub and those ash-cans."

"Well, hardly."

"And you look at the moon through that dirty skylight?"

"No! There's nothing in that old stuff. Everybody's fed up on the moon."

"It's a snug place," I said. And I came away.

I circled the stairs into the denser smell which, by this time, I found rather agreeable. The embalmer's door was open. In the gloom inside I saw the apprentice busied in some dark employment. "I got somethin' to show you," he called.

"Tomorrow," I answered.

As I was opening the street door, a woman came up

the steps.   She was a dark, Bulgarian sort of woman.
Or Esthonian, perhaps.   I held back the door to let
her pass.   She wore long ear-rings.   Her skirt was
looped high in scollops.   She wore sandals—and
painted stockings.

Autumn Days.

IT was rather a disservice when the poet wrote that the melancholy days were come. His folly is inexplicable. If he had sung through his nose of thaw and drizzle, all of us would have pitched in to help him in his dismal chorus. But October and November are brisk and cheerful months.

In the spring, to be sure, there is a languid sadness. Its beauty is too frail. Its flowerets droop upon the plucking. Its warm nights, its breeze that blows from the fragrant hills, warn us how brief is the blossom time. In August the year slumbers. Its sleepy days nod across the heavy orchards and the yellow grain fields. Smoke looks out from chimneys, but finds no wind for comrade. For a penny it would stay at home and doze upon the hearth, to await a playmate from the north. The birds are still. Only the insects sing. A threshing-machine, far off, sinks to as drowsy a melody as theirs, like a company of grasshoppers, but with longer beard and deeper voice. The streams that frolicked to nimble tunes in May now crawl from pool to pool. The very shadows linger under cover. They crouch close beneath shed and tree, and scarcely stir a finger until the fiery sun has turned its back.

September rubs its eyes. It hears autumn, as it were, pounding on its bedroom door, and turns for

another wink of sleep. But October is awakened by
the frost. It dresses itself in gaudy color. It flings
a scarlet garment on the woods and a purple scarf
across the hills. The wind, at last, like a merry piper,
cries out the tune, and its brisk and sunny days come
dancing from the north.

Yesterday was a holiday and I went walking in the
woods. Although it is still September it grows late,
and there is already a touch of October in the air.
After a week of sultry weather—a tardy remnant
from last month—a breeze yesterday sprang out of
the northwest. Like a good housewife it swept the
dusty corners of the world. It cleared our path
across the heavens and raked down the hot cobwebs
from the sky. Clouds had yawned in idleness. They
had sat on the dull circle of the earth like fat old men
with drooping chins, but yesterday they stirred themselves. The wind whipped them to their feet. It pur-
sued them and plucked at their frightened skirts. It
is thus, after the sleepy season, that the wind practices
for the rough and tumble of November. It needs but
to quicken the tempo into sixteenth notes, to rouse a
wholesome tempest.

Who could be melancholy in so brisk a month? The
poet should hang his head for shame at uttering such
a libel. These dazzling days could hale him into court.
The jury, with one voice, without rising from its box,
would hold for a heavy fine. Apples have been
gathered in. There is a thirsty, tipsy smell from the
cider presses. Hay is pitched up to the very roof.

Bursting granaries show their golden produce at the cracks. The yellow stubble of the fields is a promise that is kept. And who shall say that there is any sadness in the fallen leaves? They are a gay and sounding carpet. Who dances here needs no bell upon his ankle, and no fiddle for the tune.

And sometimes in October the air is hazy and spiced with smells. Nature, it seems, has cooked a feast in the heat of summer, and now its viands stand out to cool.

November lights its fires and brings in early candles. This is the season when chimneys must be tightened for the tempest. Their mighty throats roar that all is strong aloft. Dogs now leave a stranger to go his way in peace, and they bark at the windy moon. Windows rattle, but not with sadness. They jest and chatter with the blast. They gossip of storms on barren mountains.

Night, for so many months, has been a timid creature. It has hid so long in gloomy cellars while the regal sun strutted on his way. But now night and darkness put their heads together for his overthrow. In shadowy garrets they mutter their discontent and plan rebellion. They snatch the fields by four o'clock. By five they have restored their kingdom. They set the stars as guardsmen of their rule.

Now travelers are pelted into shelter. Signboards creak. The wind whistles for its rowdy company. Night, the monarch, rides upon the storm.

A match! We'll light the logs. We'll crack nuts

and pass the cider.   How now, master poet, is there no
thirsty passage in your throat?   I offer you a bowl of
milk and popcorn.   Must you brood tonight upon the
barren fields—the meadows brown and sear?   Who
cares now how the wind grapples with the chimneys?
Here is snug company, warm and safe.   Here are
syrup and griddle-cakes.   Do you still suck your melancholy pen when such a feast is going forward?

On Finding a Plot.

A YOUNG author has confessed to me that lately, in despair at hitting on a plot, he locked himself in his room after breakfast with an oath that he would not leave it until something was contrived and under way. He did put an apple and sandwich prudently at the back of his desk, but these, he swore, like the locusts and wild honey in the wilderness, should last him through his struggle. By a happy afterthought he took with him into retirement a volume of De Maupassant. Perhaps, he considered, if his own invention lagged and the hour grew late, he might shift its characters into new positions. Rather than starve till dawn he could dress a courtezan in honest cloth, or tease a happy wife from her household in the text to a mad elopement. Or by jiggling all the plots together, like the bits of glass in a kaleidoscope, the pieces might fall into strange and startling patterns.

This is not altogether a new thought with him. While sucking at his pen in a former drouth he considered whether a novel might not be made by combining the characters of one story with the circumstance of another. Let us suppose, for example, that Carmen, before she got into that ugly affair with the Toreador, had settled down in Barchester beneath the towers. Would the shadow of the cloister, do you

think, have cooled her southern blood? Would she
have conformed to the decent gossip of the town? Or,
on the contrary, does not a hot color always tint the
colder mixture? Suppose that Carmen came to live
just outside the Cathedral close and walked every
morning with her gay parasol and her pretty swishing
skirts past the Bishop's window.

We can fancy his pen hanging dully above his ser-
mon, with his eyes on space for any wandering
thought, as if the clouds, like treasure ships upon a
sea, were freighted with riches for his use. The
Bishop is brooding on an address to the Ladies' Sew-
ing Guild. He must find a text for his instructive
finger. It is a warm spring morning and the daffodils
are waving in the borders of the grass. A robin sings
in the hedge with an answer from his mate. There is
wind in the tree-tops with lively invitation to adventure, but the Bishop is bent to his sober task. Carmen
picks her way demurely across the puddles in the
direction of the Vicarage. Her eyes turn modestly
toward his window. Surely she does not see him at
his desk. That dainty inch of scarlet stocking is quite
by accident. It is the puddles and the wind frisking
with her skirt.

"Eh! Dear me!" The good man is merely human.
He pushes up his spectacles for nearer sight. He
draws aside the curtain. "Dear me! Bless my soul!
Who is the lady? Quite a foreign air. I don't re-
member her at our little gatherings for the heathen."
A text is forgotten. The clouds are empty caravels.

He calls to Betsy, the housemaid, for a fresh neck-cloth and his gaiters. He has recalled a meeting with the Vicar and goes out whistling softly, to disaster.

Alas! In my forgetfulness I have skimmed upon the actual plot. You have recalled already how La Signora Madeline descended on the Bishop's Palace. Her beauty was a hard assault. Except for her crippled state she might herself have toppled the Bishop over. But she pales beside the dangerous Carmen.

Suppose, for a better example, that the cheerful Mark Tapley who always came out strong in adversity, were placed in a modern Russian novel. As the undaunted Taplovitch he would have shifted its gloom to a sunny ending. Fancy our own dear Pollyanna, the glad girl, adopted by an aunt in "Crime and Punishment." Even Dostoyevsky must have laid down his doleful pen to give her at last a happy wedding—flower-girls and angel-food, even a shrill soprano behind the hired palms and a table of cut glass.

Oliver Twist and Nancy,—merely acquaintances in the original story,—with a fresh hand at the plot, might have gone on a bank holiday to Margate. And been blown off shore. Suppose that the whole excursion was wrecked on Treasure Island and that everyone was drowned except Nancy, Oliver and perhaps the trombone player of the ship's band, who had blown himself so full of wind for fox-trots on the upper deck that he couldn't sink. It is Robinson Crusoe, lodging as a handsome bachelor on the lonely island,—observe

the cunning of the plot!—who battles with the waves
and rescues Nancy. The movie-rights alone of this
are worth a fortune. And then Crusoe, Oliver, Friday and the trombone player stand a siege from John
Silver and Bill Sikes, who are pirates, with Spanish
doubloons in a hidden cove. And Crusoe falls in love
with Nancy. Here is a tense triangle. But youth
goes to youth. Crusoe's whiskers are only dyed their
glossy black. The trombone player, by good luck
(you see now why he was saved from the wreck), is
discovered to be a retired clergyman—doubtless a
Methodist. The happy knot is tied. And then—a
sail! A sail! Oliver and Nancy settle down in a semi-
detached near London, with oyster shells along the
garden path and cat-tails in the umbrella jar. The
story ends prettily under their plane-tree at the rear—
tea for three, with a trombone solo, and the faithful
Friday and Old Bill, reformed now, as gardener,
clipping together the shrubs against the sunny wall.

Was there a serpent in the garden at peaceful Cran-
ford? Suppose that one of the gay rascals of Dumas,
with tall boots and black moustachios, had got in when
the tempting moon was up. Could the gentle ladies
in their fragile guard of crinoline have withstood this
French assault?

Or Camille, perhaps, before she took her cough,
settled at Bath and entangled Mr. Pickwick in the
Pump Room. Do not a great hat and feather find
their victim anywhere? Is not a silken ankle as potent
at Bath as in Bohemia? Surely a touch of age and

gout is no prevention against the general plague. Nor
does a bald head tower above the softer passions.
Camille's pretty nose is powdered for the onslaught.
She has arranged her laces in dangerous hazard to the
eye. And now the bold huzzy undeniably winks at
Mr. Pickwick over her pint of "killibeate." She drops
her fan with usual consequence. A nod. A smile.
A word. At the Assembly—mark her sudden progress and the triumphant end!—they sit together in
the shadows of the balcony. "My dear," says Mr.
Pickwick, gazing tenderly through his glasses, "my
love, my own, will you—bless my soul!—will you
share my lodgings at Mrs. Bardell's in Goswell
Street?" We are mariners, all of us, coasting in dangerous waters. It is the syren's voice, her white
beauty gleaming on the shoal—it is the moon that
throws us on the rocks.

And then a dozen dowagers breed the gossip.
Duchesses, frail with years, pop and burst with the
pleasant secret. There is even greater commotion
than at Mr. Pickwick's other disturbing affair with
the middle-aged lady in the yellow curl-papers. This
previous affair you may recall. He had left his watch
by an oversight in the taproom, and he went down to
get it when the inn was dark. On the return he took a
false direction at the landing and, being misled by the
row of boots along the hall, he entered the wrong
room. He was in his nightcap in bed when, peeping
through the curtains, he saw the aforesaid lady brushing her back hair. A duel was narrowly averted when

this startling scandal came to the ears of the lady's lover, Mr. Peter Magnus. Camille, I think, could have kept this sharper scandal to herself. At most, with a prudent finger on her lips, she would have whispered the intrigue harmlessly behind her fan and set herself to snare a duke.

I like to think, also, of the incongruity of throwing Rollo (Rollo the perfect, the Bayard of the nursery, the example of our suffering childhood)—Rollo grown up, of course, and without his aseptic Uncle George—into the gay scandal, let us say, of the Queen's Necklace. Perhaps it is forgotten how he and his little sister Jane went to the Bull Fight in Rome on Sunday morning by mistake. They were looking for the Presbyterian Church, and hand in hand they followed the crowd. It is needless to remind you how Uncle George was vexed. Rollo was a prig. He loved his Sunday school and his hour of piano practice. He brushed his hair and washed his face without compulsion. He even got in behind his ears. He went to bed cheerfully upon a hint. Thirty years ago—I was so pestered—if I could have met Rollo in the flesh I would have lured him to the alleyway behind our barn and pushed him into the manure-pit. In the crisp vernacular of our street, I would have punched the everlasting tar out of him.

It was circumstance that held the Bishop and Rollo down. Isn't Cinderella just a common story of sordid realism until the fairy godmother appears? Except for the pumpkin and a very small foot she would have

married the butcher's boy, and been snubbed by her
sisters to the end. It was only luck that it was a
prince who awakened the Sleeping Beauty. The
plumber's assistant might have stumbled by. What
was Aladdin without his uncle, the magician? Do
princesses still sleep exposed to a golden kiss? Are
there lamps for rubbing, discarded now in attics?

Sinbad, with a steady wife, would have stayed at
home and become an alderman. Romeo might have
married a Montague and lived happily ever after. It
was but chance that Titania awakened in the Ass's
company—chance that Viola was cast on the coast of
Illyria and found her lover. Any of these plots could
have been altered by jogging the author's elbow. A
bit of indigestion wrecks the crimson shallop.
Comedy or tragedy is but the falling of the dice. By
the flip of a coin comes the poisoned goblet or the
princess.

But my young author's experiment with De
Maupassant was not successful. He tells me that
hunger caught him in the middle of the afternoon, and
that he went forth for a cup of malted milk, which is
his weakness. His head was as empty as his stomach.

And yet there are many novels written and even
published, and most of them seem to have what pass
for plots. Bipeds, undeniably, are set up with some
likeness to humanity. They talk from page to page
without any squeak of bellows. They live in lodgings
and make acquaintance across the air-shaft. They
wrestle with villains. They fall in love. They starve

and then grow famous. And at last, in all good books,
journeys end in lovers' meeting. It is as easy as lying.
Only a plot is needed.

And may not anyone set up the puppets? Rich
man, poor man, beggarman, thief! You have only to
say *eenie meenie* down the list, and trot out a brunette
or a blonde. There is broadcloth in the tiring-box,
and swords and velvet; and there is, also, patched
wool, and shiny elbows. Your lady may sigh her soul
to the Grecian tents, or watch for honest Tom on his
motor-cycle. On Venetian balcony and village stoop
the stars show alike for lovers and everywhere there
are friendly shadows in the night.

Like a master of marionettes, we may pull the
puppets by their strings. It is such an easy matter—
if once a plot is given—to lift a beggar or to overthrow
a rascal. A virtuous puppet can be hoisted to a tinsel
castle. A twitching of the thumb upsets the wicked
King. Rollo is pitched to his knees before a scheming
beauty. And would it not be fun to dangle before the
Bishop that little Carmen figure with her daring lace
and scarlet stockings?—or to swing the bold Camille
by the strings into Mr. Pickwick's arms as the curtain
falls?

Was it not Hawthorne who died leaving a notebook full of plots? And Walter Scott, when that
loyal, harassed hand of his was shriveled into death,
must have had by him a hundred hints for projected
books. One author—I forget who he was—be-
queathed to another author—the name has escaped

me—a memorandum of characters and events. At any author's death there must be a precious salvage. Among the surviving papers there sits at least one dusty heroine waiting for a lover. Here are notes for the Duchess's elopement. Here is a sketch how the deacon proved to be a villain. As old ladies put by scraps of silk for a crazy quilt, shall not an author, also, treasure in his desk shreds of character and odds and ends to make a plot?

Now the truth is, I suspect, that the actual plot has little to do with the merits of a great many of the best books. It is only the bucket that fetches up the water from the well. It is the string that holds the shining beads. Who really cares whether Tom Jones married Sophia? And what does it matter whether Falstaff died in bed or in his boots, or whether Uncle Toby married the widow? It is the mirth and casual adventure by the way that hold our interest.

Some of the best authors, indeed, have not given a thought to their plots until it is time to wind up the volume. When Dickens sent the Pickwick Club upon its travels, certainly he was not concerned whether Tracy Tupman found a wife. He had not given a thought to Sam's romance with the pretty housemaid at Mr. Nupkins's. The elder Mrs. Weller's fatal cough was clearly a happy afterthought. Thackeray, at the start, could hardly have foreseen Esmond's marriage. When he wrote the early chapters of "Vanity Fair," he had not traced Becky to her shabby garret of the Elephant at Pumpernickel. Dumas, I have no doubt, wrote from page to page, careless of the end. Doubtless he marked Milady for a bad end, but was unconcerned whether it would be a cough or noose. Victor Hugo did no more than follow a trail across the mountains of his invention, content with the kingdoms of each new turning.

In these older and more deliberate books, if a young lady smiled upon the hero, it was not already schemed whether they would be lovers, with the very manner of his proposal already set. The glittering moon was not yet bespoken for the night. "My dear young lady," this older author thinks, "you have certainly very pretty eyes and I like the way that lock of brown hair rests against your ear, but I am not at all sure that I shall let you marry my hero. Please sit around for a dozen chapters while I observe you. I must see you in tweed as well as silk. Perhaps you have an ugly habit of whining. Or safe in a married state you might wear a mob-cap in to breakfast. I'll send my hero up to London for his fling. There is an actress I must have him meet. I'll let him frolic through the winter. On his return he may choose between you."

"My dear madam," another of these older authors meditates, "how can I judge you on a first acquaintance? Certainly you talk loosely for an honest wife. It is too soon, as yet, to know how far your flirtation leads. I must observe you with Mr. Fopling in the garden after dinner. If, later, I grow dull and my readers nod, your elopement will come handy."

Nor was a lady novelist of the older school less deliberate. When a bold adventurer appears, she holds her heroine to the rearward of her affection. "I'll make no decision yet for Lady Emily," she thinks. "This gay fellow may have a wife somewhere. His smooth manner with the ladies comes with practice. It is soon enough if I decide upon their affair in my second volume. Perhaps, after all, the captain may prove to be the better man."

And yet this spacious method requires an ample genius. A smaller writer must take a map and put his finger beforehand on his destination. When a hero fares forth singing in the dawn, the author must know at once his snug tavern for the night. The hazard of the morning has been matched already with a peaceful twilight. The seeds of time are planted, the very harvest counted when the furrow's made. My heart goes out to that young author who sits locked in his study, munching his barren apple. He must perfect his scenario before he starts. How easy would be his task, if only he could just begin, "Once upon a time," and follow his careless contrivance.

I know a teacher who has a full-length novel unpublished and concealed. Sometimes, I fancy, at midnight, when his Latin themes are marked, he draws forth its precious pages. He alters and smooths his sentences while the household sleeps. And even in his classroom, as he listens to the droning of a conjugation, he leaps to horse. Little do his students suspect, as they stutter with their verbs, that with

their teacher, heedless of convention, rides the dark
lady of his swift adventure.

I look with great awe on an acquaintance who
averages more than one story a week and publishes
them in a periodical called *Frisky Stories*. He shifts
for variety among as many as five or six pen-names.
And I marvel at a friend who once wrote a story a day
for a newspaper syndicate. But his case was pathetic.
When I saw him last, he was sitting on a log in the
north forest, gloomily estimating how many of his
wretched stories would cover the wood-pulp of the
state. His health was threatened. He was resting
from the toil

> "Of dropping buckets into empty wells,
> And growing old in drawing nothing up."

From all this it must appear that the real difficulty
is in finding a sufficient plot. The start of a plot is
easy, but it is hard to carry it on and end it. I myself,
on any vacant morning, could get a hero tied hand and
foot inside a cab, but then I would not know where
to drive him. I have thought, in an enthusiastic
moment, that he might be lowered down a manhole
through the bottom of the cab. This is an unprece-
dented villainy, and I have gone so far as to select a
lonely manhole in Gramercy Park around the corner
from the Players' Club. But I am lost how my hero
could be rescued. Covered with muck, I could hardly
hope that his lady would go running to his arms. I

have, also, a pretty pencil for a fight in the ancient style, with swords upon a stairway. But what then? And what shall I do with the gallant Percival de Vere, after he has slid down the rope from his beetling dungeon tower? As for ladies—I could dress up the pretty creatures, but would they move or speak upon my bidding? No one would more gladly throw a lady and gentleman on a desert island. At a pinch I flatter myself I could draw a roaring lion. But in what circumstance should the hungry cannibals appear? These questions must tax a novelist heavily.

Or might I not, for copy, strip the front from that building opposite?

"The whole of the frontage shaven sheer,
The inside gaped: exposed to day,
Right and wrong and common and queer,
Bare, as the palm of your hand, it lay."

Every room contains a story. That chair, the stove, the very tub for washing holds its secrets. The stairs echo with the tread of a dozen lives. And in every crowd upon the street I could cast a stone and find a hero. There is a seamstress somewhere, a locksmith, a fellow with a shovel. I need but the genius to pluck out the heart of their mystery. The rumble of the subway is the friction of lives that rub together. The very roar of cities is the meshing of our human gear.

I dream of this world I might create. In romantic mood, a castle lifts its towers into the blue dome of heaven. I issue in spirit with Jeanne d'Arc from the gate of Orleans, and I play the tragedy with changing scene until the fires of Rouen have fallen into ashes. I sail the seas with Raleigh. I scheme with the hump-backed Richard. Out of the north, with wind and sunlight, my hero comes singing to his adventures.

It would be glorious fun to create a world, to paint a valley in autumn colors and set up a village at the crossroads. Housewives chatter at their wash-lines. Wheels rattle on the wooden bridge. Old men doze on the grocery bench. And now let's throw the plot, at a hazard, around the lovely Susan, the grocer's clerk. For her lover we select a young garage-man, the jest of the village, who tinkers at an improvement of a carburetor. The owner of a thousand acres on the hill shall be our villain—a wastrel and a gambler. There is a mortgage on his acres. He is pressed for payment. He steals the garage-man's blueprints. And now it is night. Susan dearly loves a movie. The Orpheum is eight miles off. Painted Cupids. Angels with trumpets. The villain. An eight-cylindered runabout. Susan. B-r-r-r-r! The movie. The runabout again. A lonely road. Just a kiss, my pretty girl. Help! Help! Chug! Chug! Aha! Foiled! The garage-man. You cur! You hound! Take that! And that! Susan. The garage-man. The blueprints. Name the happy day. Oh, joy! Oh, bliss!

It would be fun to model these little worlds and set them up to cool.

Is it any wonder that there are a million stars across the night? God Himself enjoyed the vast creation of His worlds. It was the evening and the morning of the sixth day when He set his puppets moving in their stupendous comedy.

Circus Days.

THERE have been warm winds out of the south for several days, soft rains have teased the daffodils into blossom along the fences, and this morning I heard the first clicking of a lawn-mower. It seems but yesterday that winter was tugging at the chimneys, that March freshets were brawling in the gutters; but, with the shifting of the cock upon the steeple, the spring comes from its hiding in the hills. At this moment, to prove the changing of the season, a street organ plays beneath my window. It is a rather miserable box and is stocked with senti-mental tunes for coaxing nickels out of pity. Its in-laid mahogany is soiled with travel. It has a peg-leg and it hangs around the musician's neck as if weary of the road. "Master," it seems to say, "may we sit awhile? My old stump is wearing off." And yet on this warm morning in the sunlight there is almost a touch of frolic in the box. A syncopation attempts a happier temper. It has sniffed the fragrant air, and desires to put a better face upon its troubles.

The housemaid next door hangs out the Monday's garments to dry, and there is a pleasant flapping of legs and arms as if impatient for partners in a dance. Must a petticoat sit unasked when the music plays? Surely breeches and stockings will not hold back when a lively skirt shall beckon. A slow waltz might even tempt aunty's nightgown off the line. If only a vegetable man would come with a cart of red pieplant and green lettuce and offer his gaudy wares along the street, then the evidence of spring would be complete.

But there is even better evidence at hand. This morning I noticed that a circus poster had been pasted on the billboard near the school-house. Several children and I stopped to see the wonders that were promised. Then the school-bell rang and they dawdled off. At Stratford, also, once upon a time, boys with shining morning faces crept like snails to school. Were there circus billboards in so remote a day? The pundits, bleared with search, are strangely silent. This morning it will be a shrewd lesson that keeps the children's thoughts from leaping out the window. Two times two will hardly hold their noses on the desk.

On the billboard there is the usual blonde with pink legs, balanced on one toe on a running horse. The clown holds the paper hoop. The band is blowing

itself very red in the face. An acrobat leaps headlong
from a high trapeze. There are five rings, thirty
clowns, an amazing variety of equestrian and slack-
wire genius, a galaxy of dazzling beauties; and every
performance includes a dizzy, death-defying dive by
a dauntless dare-devil—on a bicycle from the top of
the tent. And of course there are elephants and per-
forming dogs and fat ladies. One day only—two
performances—rain or shine.

Does not this kind of billboard stir the blood in
these languid days of spring? It is a tonic to the sober
street. It is a shining dial that marks the coming of
the summer. In the winter let barns and fences proclaim the fashion of our dress and tease us with bar-
gains for the kitchen. But in the spring, when the
wind is from the south, fences have a better use. They
announce the circus. What child now will not come
upon a trot? What student can keep to his solemn
book? There is a sleepy droning from the school-
house. The irregular verbs—lawless rascals with a
past—chafe in a dull routine. The clock loiters
through the hour.

It was by mere coincidence that last night on my
way home I stopped at a news-stand for a daily paper,
and saw a periodical by the name of the *Paste-Brush*.
On a gay cover was the picture of another blonde—a
sister, maybe, of the lady of the billboard. She was
held by an ankle over a sea of upturned faces, but by
her happy, inverted smile she seemed unconscious of
her danger.

The *Paste-Brush* is new to me. I bought a copy, folded its scandalous' cover out of sight and took it home. It proves to be the trade journal of the circus and amusement-park interests. It announces a circulation of seventy thousand, which I assume is largely among acrobats, magicians, fat ladies, clowns, liniment-venders, lion-tamers, Caucasian Beauties and actors on obscure circuits.

Now it happens that among a fairly wide acquaintance I cannot boast a single acrobat or liniment-vender. Nor even a professional fat man. A friend of mine, it is true, swells in that direction as an amateur, but he rolls night and morning as a corrective. I did once, also, pass an agreeable hour at a County Fair with a strong man who bends iron bars in his teeth. He had picked me from his audience as one of convincing weight to hang across the bar while he performed his trick. When the show was done, he introduced me to the Bearded Beauty and a talkative Mermaid from Chicago. One of my friends, also, has told me that she is acquainted with a lady—a former pupil of her Sunday school—who leaps on holidays in the park from a parachute. The bantam champion, too, many years ago, lived behind us around the corner; but he was a distant hero, sated with fame, unconscious of our youthful worship. But these meetings are exceptional and accidental. Most of us, let us assume, find our acquaintance in the usual walks of life. Last night, therefore, having laid by the letters of Madame d'Arblay, on whose seven volumes I have

been engaged for a month, I took up the *Paste-Brush*
and was carried at once into another and unfamiliar
world.

The frontispiece is the big tent of the circus with
side-shows in the foreground. There is a great wheel
with its swinging baskets, a merry-go-round, a Funny
Castle, and a sword-swallower's booth. By a dense
crowd around a wagon I am of opinion that here
nothing less than red lemonade is sold. Certainly
Jolly Maude, "that mountain of flesh," holds a distant,
surging crowd against the ropes.

An article entitled "Freaks I Have Known" is
worth the reading. You may care to know that a cele-
brated missing-link—I withhold the lady's name—
plays solitaire in her tent as she waits her turn.
Bearded ladies, it is asserted, are mostly married and
have a fondness for crocheting out of hours. A certain three-legged boy, "the favorite of applauding
thousands," tried to enlist for the war, but was rejected because he broke up a pair of shoes. The Wild
Man of Borneo lived and died in Waltham, Massa-
chusetts. If the street and number were given, it
would tempt me to a pilgrimage. Have I not journeyed to Concord and to Plymouth? Perhaps an old
inhabitant—an antique spinster or rheumatic grocer
—can still remember the pranks of the Wild Man's
childhood.

But in the *Paste-Brush* the pages of advertisement
are best. Slot machines for chewing-gum are offered
for sale—Merry-Widow swings, beach babies (a kind

of doll), genuine Tiffany rings that defy the expert, second-hand saxophones, fountain pens at eight cents each and sofa pillows with pictures of Turkish beauties.

But let us suppose that you, my dear sir, are one of those seventy thousand subscribers and are by profession a tattooer. On the day of publication with what eagerness you scan its columns! Here is your opportunity to pick up an improved outfit—"stencils and supplies complete, with twelve chest designs and a picture of a tattooed lady in colors, twelve by eighteen, for display. Send for price list." Or if you have skill in charming snakes and your stock of vipers is running low, write to the Snake King of Florida for his catalogue. "He treats you right." Here is an advertisement of an alligator farm. Alligator-wrestlers, it is said, make big money at popular resorts on the southern circuit. You take off your shoes and stockings, when the crowd has gathered, and wade into the slimy pool. It needs only a moderate skill to seize the fierce creature by his tail and haul him to the shore. A deft movement throws him on his back. Then you tickle him under the ear to calm him and pass the hat.

Here in the *Paste-Brush* is an announcement of a ship-load of monkeys from Brazil. Would you care to buy a walrus? A crocodile is easy money on the Public Square in old-home week. Or perhaps you are a glass-blower with your own outfit, a ventriloquist, a diving beauty, a lyric tenor or a nail-eater. If so, here is an agent who will book you through the West. The small cities and large towns of Kansas yearn for you. Or if you, my dear madam, are of good figure, the Alamo Beauties, touring in Mississippi, want your services. Long season. No back pay.

Would you like to play a tuba in a ladies' orchestra? You are wanted in Oklahoma. The Sunshine Girls— famous on western circuits—are looking to augment their number. "Wanted: Woman for Eliza and Ophelia. Also a child for Eva. Must double as a pony. State salary. Canada theatres."

It is affirmed that there is money in box-ball, that hoop-la yields a fortune, that "you mop up the tin" with a huckley-buck. It sounds easy. I wonder what a huckley-buck is like. I wonder if I have ever seen one. It must be common knowledge to the readers of the *Paste-Brush,* for the term is not explained. Perhaps one puts a huckley-buck in a wagon and drives from town to town. Doubtless it returns a fortune in a County Fair. Is this not an opportunity for an underpaid school-teacher or slim seamstress? No longer must she subsist upon a pittance. Here is rest for her blue, old fingers. Let her write today for a catalogue. She should choose a huckley-buck of gaudy color, with a Persian princess on the side, to draw the crowd. Let her stop by the village pump and sound a stirring blast upon her megaphone.

Or perhaps you, my dear sir, have been chafing in an indoor job. You have been hooped through a dreary winter upon a desk. If so, your gloomy disposition can be mended by a hoop-la booth, whatever it is. "This way, gentlemen! Try your luck! Positively no blanks. A valuable prize for everybody." Your stooped shoulders will straighten. Your digestion will come to order in a month. Or why not run a stand at the beach for walking-sticks, with a view in the handle of a "dashing French actress in a daring pose, or the latest picture of President and Mrs. Wilson at the Peace Conference."

Or curiosities may be purchased—"two-headed giants, mermaids, sea-serpents, a devil-child and an Egyptian mummy. New lists ready." A mummy would be a quiet and profitable companion for our seamstress in the long vacation. It would need less attention than a sea-serpent. She should announce the dusty creature as the darling daughter of the Ptolemies. When the word has gone round, she may sit at ease before the booth in scarlet overalls and count the dropping nickels. With what vigor will she take to her thimble in the autumn!

Out in Gilmer, Texas, there is a hog with six legs— "alive and healthy. Five hundred dollars take it." Here is a merchant who will sell you "snake, frog and monkey tights." After your church supper, on the stage of the Sunday school, surely, in such a costume, my dear madam, you could draw a crowd. Study the trombone and double your income. Can you yodle? "It can be learned at home, evenings, in six easy lessons."

A used popcorn engine is cut in half. A waffle machine will be shipped to you on trial. Does no one wish to take the road with a five-legged cow? Here is one for sale—an extraordinary animal that cleaned up sixty dollars in one afternoon at a County Fair in Indiana. "Walk up, ladies and gentlemen! The marvel of the age. Plenty of time before the big show starts. A five-legged cow. Count 'em. Answers to the name of Guenevere. Shown before all the crowned heads of Europe. Once owned by the Czar of Russia. Only a dime. A tenth of a dollar. Ten cents. Show about to start."

Or perhaps you think it more profitable to buy a steam calliope—some very good ones are offered second-hand in the *Paste-Brush*—and tour your neighboring towns. Make a stand at the crossroads under the soldiers' monument. Give a free concert. Then when the crowd is thick about you, offer them a magic ointment. Rub an old man for his rheumatism. Throw away his crutch, clap him on the back and pronounce him cured. Or pull teeth for a dollar each. It takes but a moment for a diagnosis. When once the fashion starts, the profitable bicuspids will drop around you.

And Funny Castles can be bought. Perhaps you do not know what they are. They are usual in amusement parks. You and a favorite lady enter, hand in hand. It is dark inside and if she is of an agreeable timidity she leans to your support. Only if you are a

churl will you deny your arm. Then presently a fiery
devil's head flashes beside you in the passage. The
flooring tilts and wobbles as you step. Here, surely,
no lady will wish to keep her independence. Presently
a picture opens in the wall. It is souls in hell, or the
Queen of Sheba on a journey. Then a sharp draft
ascends through an opening in the floor. Your lady
screams and minds her skirts. A progress through a
Funny Castle, it is said, ripens the greenest friendship.
Now take the lady outside, smooth her off and regale
her with a lovers' sundae. Funny Castles, with wind
machines, a Queen of Sheba almost new, and devil's
head complete, can be purchased. Remit twenty-five
per cent with order. The balance on delivery.

Perhaps I am too old for these high excitements.
Funny Castles are behind me. Ladies of the circus,
alas! who ride in golden chariots are no longer beautiful. Cleopatra in her tinsel has sunk to the common
level. Clowns with slap-sticks rouse in me only a
moderate delight.

At this moment, as I write, the clock strikes twelve.
It is noon and school is out. There is a slamming of
desks and a rush for caps. The boys scamper on the
stairs. They surge through the gate. The acrobat
on the billboard greets their eyes—the clown, also the
lady with the pink legs. They pause. They gather in
a circle. They have fallen victims to her smile. They
mark the great day in their memory.

The wind is from the south. The daffodils flourish
along the fences. The street organ hangs heavily on

its strap.   There will be a parade in the morning.
The freaks will be on their platforms by one o'clock.
The great show starts at two.   I shall buy tickets and
take Nepos, my nephew.

In Praise of a Lawn-Mower.

I DO not recall that anyone has written the praises of a lawn-mower. I seem to sow in virgin soil. One could hardly expect a poet to lift up his voice on such a homely theme. By instinct he prefers the more rhythmic scythe. Nor, on the other hand, will mechanical folk pay a full respect to a barren engine without cylinders and motive power. But to me it is just intricate enough to engage the interest. I can trace the relation of its wheels and knives, and see how the lesser spinning starts the greater. In a printing press, on the contrary, I hear only the general rattle. Before a gas-engine, also, I am dumb. Its sixteen processes to an explosion baffle me. I could as easily digest a machine for setting type. I nod blankly, as if a god explained the motion of the stars. Even when I select a motor I take it merely on reputation and by bouncing on the cushions to test its comfort.

It has been a great many years since I was last intimate with a lawn-mower. My acquaintance began in the days when a dirty face was the badge of freedom. One early Saturday morning I was hard at work before breakfast. Mother called down through the upstairs shutters, at the first clicking of the knives, to ask if I wore my rubbers in the dew. With the money earned by noon, I went to Conrad's shop. The

season for tops and marbles had gone by. But in the
window there was a peerless baseball with a rubber
core, known as a *cock-of-the-walk*. By indecision,
even by starting for the door, I bought it a nickel off
because it was specked by flies.

It did not occur to me last week, at first, that I
could cut the grass. I talked with an Irishman who
keeps the lawn next door. He leaned on his rake, took
his pipe from his mouth and told me that his time was
full. If he had as many hands as a centipede—so he
expressed himself—he could not do all the work that
was asked of him. The whole street clamored for his
service. Then I talked with an Italian on the other
side, who comes to work on a motor-cycle with his
lawn-mower across his shoulder. His time was worth
a dollar an hour, and he could squeeze me in after
supper and before breakfast. But how can I con-
sistently write upstairs—I am puttering with a novel
—with so expensive a din sounding in my ears? My
expected royalties shrink beside such swollen pay. So
I have become my own yard-man.

Last week I had the lawn-mower sharpened, but it
came home without adjustment. It went down the
lawn without clipping a blade. What a struggle I
had as a child getting the knives to touch along their
entire length! I remember it as yesterday. What an
ugly path was left when they cut on one side only!
My bicycle chain, the front wheel that wobbled, the
ball-bearings in the gear, none of these things were so
perplexing. Last week I got out my screw-driver

with somewhat of my old feeling of impotence. I sat down on the grass with discouragement in contemplation. One set of screws had to be loosened while another set was tightened, and success lay in the delicacy of my advance. What was my amazement to discover that on a second trial my mower cut to its entire width! Even when I first wired a base-plug and found that the table lamp would really light, I was not more astonished.

This success with the lawn-mower has given me hope. I am not, as I am accused, all thumbs. I may yet become a handy man around the house. Is the swirl of furnace pipes inside my intellect? Perhaps I can fix the leaky packing in the laundry tubs, and henceforth look on the plumber as an equal brother. My dormant brain cells at last are wakened. But I must curb myself. I must not be too useful. There is no rest for a handy man. It is ignorance that permits a vacant holiday. At most I shall admit a familiarity with base-plugs and picture-wire and rubber washers—perhaps even with canvas awnings, which smack pleasantly of the sea—but I shall commit myself no further.

Once in a while I rather enjoy cleaning the garage —raking down the cobwebs from the walls and windows with a stream from the hose—puddling the dirt into the central drain. I am ruthless with old oil cans and with the discarded clothing of the chauffeur we had last month. Why is an old pair of pants stuffed so regularly in the tool drawer? There is a barrel at

the alley fence—but I shall spare the details. It was
the river Alpheus that Hercules turned through the
Augean stables. They had held three thousand oxen
and had not been cleaned for thirty years. Dear me!
I know oxen. I rank this labor ahead of the killing
of the Hydra, or fetching the golden apples of the
Hesperides. Our garage can be sweetened with a
hose.

But I really like outside work. Last week I pulled
up a quantity of dock and dandelions that were
strangling the grass. And I raked in seed. This
morning, when I went out for the daily paper, I saw
a bit of tender green. The Reds, as I noticed in the
headline of the paper, were advancing on Warsaw.
France and England were consulting for the defense
of Poland, but I ignored these great events and stood
transfixed in admiration before this shimmer of new
grass.

Our yard, fore and aft, is about an afternoon's
work. And now that I have cut it once I have signed
up for the summer. It requires just the right amount
of intelligence. I would not trust myself to pull
weeds in the garden. M—— has the necessary skill
for this. I might pull up the Canterbury bells which,
out of season, I consider unsightly stalks. And I do
not enjoy clipping the grass along the walks. It is a
kind of barber's job. But I like the long straight-
aways, and I could wish that our grass plot stretched
for another hundred feet.

And I like the sound of a lawn-mower. It is such

a busy click and whirr. It seems to work so willingly. Not even a sewing-machine has quite so brisk a tempo. And when a lawn-mower strikes a twig, it stops suddenly on its haunches with such impatience to be off again. "Bend over, won't you," it seems to say, "and pull out that stick. These trees are a pesky nuisance. They keep dropping branches all the while. Now then! Are we ready? Whee! What's an apple? I can cut an apple all to flinders. You whistle and I'll whirr. Let's run down that slope together!"

On Dropping Off to Sleep.

I SLEEP too well—that is, I go to sleep too soon. I am told that I pass a few minutes of troubled breathing—not vulgar snores, but a kind of uneasy ripple on the shore of wakefulness—then I drift out with the silent tide. Doubtless I merit no sympathy for my perfection—and yet—

Well, in the first place, lately we have had windy, moonlit nights and as my bed sets at the edge of the sleeping porch and the rail cuts off the earth, it is like a ride in an aëroplane to lie awake among the torn and ragged clouds. I have cast off the moorings of the sluggish world. Our garden with its flowering path, the coop for our neighbor's chickens, the apple tree, all have sunk from sight. The prow of my plane is pitched across the top of a waving poplar. Earth's harbor lights are at the stern. The Pleiades mark the channel to the open sky. I must hang out a lantern to fend me from the moon.

I shall keep awake for fifteen minutes, I think. Perhaps I can recall Keats's sonnet to the night:

"When I behold, upon the night's starr'd face,
　Huge cloudy symbols of a high romance—"

and those lines of Milton about the moon rising in clouded majesty, unveiling her peerless light.

Here a star peeps out. Presently its companions

will show themselves and I shall know the constellation. Are they playing like little children at hide-and-
seek? Do I catch Arcturus looking from its cover?
Shall I shout hi-spy to Alpha Lyra? A shooting star,
that has crouched behind a cloud, runs home to the
goal untagged. Surely these glistening worlds cannot
be hard-fisted planets like our own, holding a close
schedule across the sky. They have looted the shining
treasure of the sunset. They sail the high fantastic
seas like caravels blown from India. In the twilight
they have lifted vagrant anchors and they will moor
in strange havens at the dawn.

Are not these ragged clouds the garment of the
night? Like the beggar maiden of an ancient tale she
runs with flying raiment. She unmasks her beauty
when the world's asleep. And the wind, like an eager
prince upon his wooing, rides out of the stormy north.

And then! Poof! Sleep draws its dark curtain
across the glittering pageant—

Presently I hear Annie, the cook, on the kitchen
steps below, beating me up to breakfast. She sounds
her unwelcome reveille on a tin pan with an iron spoon.
Her first alarm I treat with indifference. It even
weaves itself pleasantly into my dreams. I have been
to a circus lately, let us say, and this racket seems to
be the tom-tom of a side-show where a thin gentleman
swallows snakes. Nor does a second outburst stir me.
She only tries the metal and practices for the later din.
At the third alarm I rise, for now she nurses a mighty
wrath. I must humor the angry creature lest in her

fury she push over a shelf of crockery. There is a cold jump for slippers—a chilly passage.

I passed a week lately at a country hotel where there were a number of bad sleepers—men broken by the cares of business, but convalescent. Each morning, as I dressed, I heard them on the veranda outside my window, exchanging their complaints. "Well," said one, "I slept three hours last night." "I wish I could," said a second. "I never do," said a third. No matter how little sleep the first man allowed himself, the second clipped off an hour. The third man told the bells he had heard—one and two and three and four —both Baptist and Methodist—and finished with his preceding competitor at least a half hour down. But always there was an old man—an ancient man with flowing beard—who waited until all were done, and concluded the discussion just at the breakfast gong: *"I never slept a wink."* This was the perfect score. His was the golden cup. Whereupon the insomnious veranda hung its defeated head with shame, and filed into the dining-room to be soothed and comforted with griddle-cakes.

This daily contest recalled to me the story of the two men drowned in the Dayton and Johnstown floods who boasted to each other when they came to heaven. Has the story gone the rounds? For a while they were the biggest lions among all the angels, and harps hung untuned and neglected in their presence. As often as they met in the windy portico of heaven, one of these heroes, falling to reminiscence of the flood that drowned him, lifted the swirling water of Johnstown to the second floor. The other hero, not to be outdone, drenched the Dayton garrets. The first was now compelled to submerge a chimney. Turn by turn they mounted in competition to the top of familiar steeples. But always an old man sat by—an ancient man with flowing beard—who said "Fudge!" in a tone of great contempt. Must I continue? Surely you have guessed the end. It was the old mariner himself. It was the survivor of Ararat. It was Noah. Once, I myself, among these bad sleepers on the veranda, boasted that I had heard the bells at two o'clock, but I was scorned as an unfledged novice in their high convention.

Sleeping too well seems to argue that there is nothing on your mind. Your head, it is asserted by the jealous, is a vacancy that matches the empty spaces of the night. It is as void as the untwinkling north. If there has been a rummage, they affirm, of important matters all day above your ears, it can hardly be checked at once by popping the tired head down upon a pillow. These fizzing squibs of thought cannot be smothered in a blanket. When one has planned a railroad or a revolution, the mighty churning still progresses in the dark. A dubious franchise must be gained. Villains must be pricked down for execution. Or bankers have come up from Paraguay, and one meditates from hour to hour on the sureness of the loan. Or perhaps an imperfect poem searches for a rhyme, or the plot of a novel sticks.

It is the shell, they say, which is fetched from the stormy sea that roars all night. My head, alas, by the evidence, is a shell which is brought from a stagnant shore.

Tired Nature's sweet restorer, balmy sleep! Sleep that knits up the ravell'd sleave of care! That is all very well, and pretty poetry, but I am afraid, when everything is said, that I am a sleepy-head. I do not, of course, have to pinch myself at a business meeting. At high noon I do not hear the lotus song. I do not topple, full of dreams, off the platform of a street-car. The sleepy poppy is not always at my nose.

Nor do I yawn at dinner behind a napkin, or doze in the firelight when there are guests about. My manners keep me from this boorishness. In an extremity, if they sit too late, I stir the fire, or I put my head out of doors for the wind to waken me. I show a sudden anxiety whether the garage is locked. I pretend that the lawn-mower is left outside, or that the awnings are loose and flapping. But I do not dash out the lights when our guests are still upon the steps. I listen at the window until I hear their motor clear the corner. Then I turn furiously to my buttons. I kick off my shoes upon the staircase.

Several of us were camping once in the woods north of Lake Superior. As we had no guides we did all the work ourselves, and everyone was of harder endurance than myself. Was it not Pippa who cried out "Morning's at seven"? Seven! I look on her as being no better than a slug-a-bed. She should have had her dishes washed and been on her way by six. Our day began at five. Our tents had to be taken down, our blankets and duffle packed. We were regularly on the water an hour before Pippa stirred a foot. And then there were four or five hours of paddling, perhaps in windy water. And then a new camp was made. Our day matched the exertions of a traveling circus. In default of expert knowledge I carried water, cut brouse for the beds and washed dishes. Little jobs, of an unpleasant nature, were found for me as often as I paused. Others did the showy, light-fingered work. I was housemaid and roustabout from sunrise to weary sunset. I was never allowed to rest. Nor was I permitted to flop the bacon, which I consider an easy, sedentary occupation. I acquired, unjustly,—let us agree in this!—a reputation for laziness, because one day I sat for several hours in a blueberry patch, when work was going forward.

And then one night, when all labor seemed done and there was an hour of twilight, I was asked to read aloud. Everyone settled himself for a feast of Shakespeare's sonnets. But it was my ill luck that I selected the sonnet that begins, "Weary with toil, I haste me to my bed." A great shout went up—a shout of derision. That night I read no more. I carried up six or eight pails of water from the spring and followed the sonneteer's example.

There are a great many books that I would like to read of a winter's evening if I could stay awake—all of the histories, certainly, of Fiske. And Rhodes, perhaps. I might even read "The Four Horsemen," "Trilby" and "The Education of Henry Adams," so as not to be alone. It is snug by the fire, and the very wind taps on the window as if it asked for invitation to share the hearth. I could compile a list, a five-foot shelf, for these nights of tempest. There is a writer in a Boston paper who tells us every week the books that he would like to read. His is a prospect rather than a review, for it is based on his anticipation. But does he ever read these books? Perhaps he, too, dozes. His book slips off his knee and his chin drops to comfort on his front. Let me inform him that a wood fire—if the logs are hardly dry—is a corrective. Its debility, as water oozes at the end, requires attendance every five minutes. Even Wardle's fat boy at Manor Farm could have lasted through the evening if the poker had been forced into his hand so often. "I read," says Tennyson, "before my eyelids dropt their shade." And wasn't Alice sitting with her book when she fell asleep and down the rabbit-hole? "And so to bed," writes Pepys. He, too, then, is one of us.

I wonder if that phrase—he who runs may read—has not a deeper significance than lies upon the surface. Perhaps the prophet—was it Habakkuk who wrote the line?—it does not matter—perhaps the bearded prophet had himself the sleepy habit, and kept moving briskly for remedy around his study. I can see him in dressing-gown and slippers, with book in hand—his whiskers veering in the wind—quickening his lively pace around the kerosene lamp, steering among the chairs, stumbling across the cat—

In ambition I am a night-hawk. I would like to sit late with old books and reconstruct the forgotten world at midnight. These bells that I hear now across the darkness are the mad bells of Saint Bartholomew. With that distant whistle—a train on the B. & O.— Guy Fawkes gathers his villains to light the fuse. Through my window from the night I hear the sounds of far-off wars and kingdoms falling.

And I would like, also, at least in theory, to sit with a merry company of friends, and let the cannikin clink till dawn.

I would like to walk the streets of our crowded city and marvel at the windows—to speculate on the thousand dramas that weave their webs in our common life. Here is mirth that shakes its sides when its neighbors sleep. Here is a hungry student whose ambition builds him rosy castles. Here is a light at a fevered pillow where hope burns dim.

On some fairy night I would wish to wander in the woods, when there are dancing shadows and a moon. Here Oberon holds state. Here Titania sleeps. I would cross a silver upland. I would stand on a barren hill-top, like the skipper of the world in its whirling voyage.

But these high accomplishments are beyond me. Habakkuk and the fat boy, and Alice and Pepys and I, and all the others, must be content. Even the wet wood and the poker fail. The very wind grows sleepy at the window. Our chins fall forward. Our books slip off our knees.

And now, at last, our buoyant bed floats among the stars. I have cast off the moorings of the sluggish world. Earth's harbor lights are at the stern. The Pleiades mark the channel to the moon—

Poof! Sleep draws again its dark curtain across the glittering pageant.

Who Was Jeremy?

WHO was Jeremy Bentham? I have run on his name recently two or three times. I could, of course, find out. The Encyclopedia—volume *Aus to Bis*—would enlighten me. Right now, downstairs in the bookcase—up near the top where the shabby books are kept—among the old Baedekers—there is a life of him by Leslie Stephen. No! That is a life of Hobbes. I don't know anything about Hobbes either. It seems to me that he wrote the "Leviathan," whatever that was. But there is a Bentham somewhere around the house. But I have not read it.

In a rough way I know who Bentham was. He lived perhaps a hundred years ago and he had a theory of utility. Utility was to clean the infected world. Even the worst of us were to rise out of the tub white and perfect. It was Bentham who wished to revisit the world in a hundred years to see how sweet and clean we had become. He was to utility what Malthus was to population. Malthus! There is another hard one. It is the kind of name that is cut round the top of a new City Hall to shame citizens by their ignorance.

I can go downstairs this minute and look up Bentham. Is it worth while? But then I might be called to dinner in the middle of the article, or I might be

wanted to move the refrigerator. There is a musty
smell, it seems, in the drain pipe, and the stubborn
casters are turned sidewise. It hardly seems worth
the chance and effort.

There are a great many things that really do stir
my curiosity, and even those things I don't look up.
Or tardily, after my ignorance has been exposed. The
other day the moon arose—as a topic—at the round
table of the club where I eat lunch. It had really
never occurred to me that we had never seen its other
side, that we never could—except by a catastrophe—
unless it smashed into a planet and was thrown heels
up. How does it keep itself so balanced that one face
is forever hid? Try to roll an apple around a pumpkin and meanwhile spin the pumpkin. Try this on
your carpet. I take my hat off to the moon.

I have been very ignorant of the moon. All of
these years I have regarded it as a kindly creature that
showed itself now and then merely on a whim. It was
just jogging around of an evening, so I supposed, and
looked us up. It was an old neighbor who dropped in
after dinner, as it were, for a bit of gossip and an
apple. But even the itinerant knife-grinder—whose
whirling wheel I can hear this minute below me in the
street—even the knife-grinder has a route. He knows
at what season we grow dull. What necessity, then,
of ours beckons to the moon? Perhaps it comes with
a silver brush to paint the earth when it grows shabby
with the traffic of the day. Perhaps it shows itself to
stir a lover who halts coldly in his suit. The pink god,

they say, shoots a dangerous arrow when the moon is full.

The extent of my general ignorance is amazing. And yet, I suppose, by persistence and energy I could mend it. Old Doctor Dwight used to advise those of us who sat in his classroom to read a hard book for half an hour each day. How those half hours would mount up through the years! What a prodigious background of history, of science, of literature, one would gain as the years revolved! If I had followed his advice I would today be bursting with knowledge of Jeremy Bentham; I would never have been tripped upon the moon.

How ignorant most of us are of the times in which we live! We see the smoke and fires of revolution in Europe. We hear the cries of famine and disease, but our perception is lost in the general smudge. How are the Balkans parceled? How is the nest of nationalities along the Danube disposed? This morning there is revolt in Londonderry. What parties are opposite in the quarrel? Trouble brews in Chile. Is Tacni-Arica a district or a mountain range? The Åland Islands breed war in the north. Today there is a casualty list from Bagdad. The Bolsheviki advance on Warsaw. Those of us who are cobblers tap our shoes unruffled, tailors stitch, we bargain in the market —all of us go about on little errands without excitement when the news is brought.

And then there is mechanics. This is now so preeminently a mechanical world that no one ought to be

entirely ignorant of cylinders and cogs and carbure-
tors.   And yet my own motor is as dark as Africa.
I am as ignorant of a carburetor as of the black
stomach of a zebra.   Once a carpenter's bench was
given me at Christmas, fitted up with all manner of
tricky tools.   The bookshelves I built in my first high
enthusiasm have now gone down to the basement to
hold the canned fruit, where they lean with rickets
against the wall.   Even the box I made to hold the
milk bottles on the back steps has gone the way of
flesh.   Any chicken-coop of mine would topple in the
wind.   Well-instructed hens would sit around on
fence-posts and cackle at my efforts with a saw.
Certainly, if a company of us were thrown on a desert
island, it would not be I who proved the Admirable
Crichton.   Not by my shrewdness could we build a
hut.   Robinson Crusoe contrived a boat.   If I tied a
raft together it would be sure to sink.

Where are the Virgin Islands?   What makes a tea-
pot bubble?   What forces bring the rain and tempest?

In cooking I go no farther than an egg.   Birds, to
me, are either sparrows or robins.   I know an elm and
a maple, but hemlocks and pines and firs mix me up.
I am not to be trusted to pull the weeds.   Up would
come the hollyhocks.   Japanese prints and Chinese
vases sit in a world above me.

I can thump myself in front without knowing
whether I jar my stomach or my liver.   I have no
notion where my food goes when it disappears.   When
once I have tilted my pudding off its spoon my knowl-

edge ceases. It is as a child of Israel on journey in the wilderness. Does it pass through my thorax? And where do my lungs branch off?

I know nothing of etchings, and I sit in gloomy silence when friends toss Whistler and Rembrandt across the table. I know who our mayor is, but I scratch my head to name our senator. And why does the world crumple up in hills and mountains?

I could look up Jeremy Bentham and hereafter I would know all about him. And I could look up the moon. And Hobbes. And Leslie Stephen, who wrote a book about him. And a man named Maitland who wrote a life of Stephen. Somebody must have written about Maitland. I could look him up, too. And I could read about the Balkans and tell my neighbors whether they are tertiary or triassic. I could pursue the thorax to its lair. Saws and chicken-coops, no doubt, are an engaging study. I might take a tree-book to the country, or seek an instructive job in a garage.

But what is the use? Right in front of Jeremy Bentham, in *Aus to Bis,* is George Bentham, an English botanist. To be thorough I would have to read about him also. Then following along is Bentivoglio, and Benzene—a long article on benzene. And Beowulf! No educated person should be quite ignorant of him. Albrecht Bitzius was a Swiss novelist. Somehow he has escaped me entirely. And Susanna Blamire, "the muse of Cumberland"! She sounds engaging. Who is there so incurious that he would not

give an evening to Borneo? And the Bryophyta?—
which I am glad to learn include "the mosses and the
liverworts." Dear me! it is quite discouraging.

And then, when I am gaining information on
Hobbes, the Hittites, right in front, take my eye.
Hilarius wrote "light verses of the goliardic type"—
whatever that means. And the hippopotamus! "the
largest representative of the non-ruminating artio-
dactyle ungulate mammals." I must sit with the
hippopotamus and worm his secret.

And after I have learned to use the saw, I would
have to take up the plane. And then the auger. And
Whistler. And Japanese prints. And a bird book.

It is very discouraging.

I stand with Pope. Certainly, unless one is very
thirsty and has a great deal of vacant time, it is best
to avoid the Pierian spring.

Jeremy can go and hang himself. I am learning to
play golf.

A Chapter for Children.

ONCE upon a time—for this is the way a story should begin—there lived in a remote part of the world a family of children whose father was busy all day making war against his enemies. And so, as their mother, also, was busy (clubs, my dear, and parties), they were taken care of and had their noses wiped—but in a most kindly way —by an old man who loved them very much.

Now this old man had been a jester in his youth. For these were the children of a king and so, of course, they had a jester, just as you and I, if we are rich, have a cook. He had been paid wages—I don't know how many kywatskies—merely to stand in the dining-room and say funny things, and nobody asked him to jump around for the salt or to hurry up the waffles. And he didn't even brush up the crumbs afterward.

I do not happen to know the children of any king— there is not a single king living on our street—yet, except for their clothes, they are much like other children. Of course they wear shinier clothes. It is not the shininess that comes from sliding down the stair rail, but a royal shininess, as though it were always eleven o'clock on Sunday morning and the second bell of the Methodist church were ringing, with several deacons on the steps. For if one's father is a king, ambassadors and generals keep dropping in all the time, and queens, dressed up in brocade so stiff you can hear them breathe.

One day the children had been sliding down hill in the snow—on Flexible Flyers, painted red—and their mittens and stockings were wet. So the old man felt their feet—tickling their toes—and set them, bare-legged, in a row, in front of the nursery fire. And he told them a story.

"O children of the king!" he began, and with that he wiped their noses all round, for it had been a cold day, when even the best-mannered persons snuffle now and then. "O children of the king!" he began again, and then he stopped to light a taper at the fire. For he was a wise old man and he knew that when there is excitement in a tale, a light will keep the bogies off. This old man could tell a story so that your eyes opened wider and wider, as they do when Annie brings in ice-cream with raspberry sauce. And once in a while he said Odd Zooks, and God-a-Mercy when he forgot himself.

"Once upon a time," he began, "there lived a king in a far-off country. To get to that country, O children of a king, you would have to turn and turn, and spell out every signpost. And then you climb up the sides of seventeen mountains, and swim twenty-three streams precisely. Here you wait till dusk. But just before the lamps are lighted, you get down on all-fours—if you are a boy (girls, I believe, don't have all-fours)—and crawl under the sofa. Keep straight on for an hour or so with the coal-scuttle three points starboard, but be careful not to let your knees touch the carpet, for that wears holes in them and spoils the magic. Then get nurse to pull you out by the hind legs—and—*there you are.*

"Once upon a time, then, there lived a king with a ferocious moustache and a great sword which rattled when he walked around the house. He made scratches all over the piano legs, but no one felt like giving him a paddy-whack. This king had a pretty daughter.

"Now it is a sad fact that there was a war going on. It was between this king who had the pretty daughter and another king who lived near by, on an adjoining farm, so to speak. And the first king had sworn by his halidome—and at this his court turned pale—that he would take his enemy by his blasted nose.

"Both of these kings lived in castles whose walls were thick and whose towers were high. And around their tops were curious indentings that looked as your teeth would look if every other one were pulled. These castles had moats with lily pads and green water in them, which was not at all healthful, except that persons in those days did not know about it and were consequently just as well off. And there were jousting fields and soup caldrons (with a barrel of animal crackers) and a tun of lemonade (six glasses to a lemon)—everything to make life comfortable.

"Here's a secret. The other king who lived near by was in love with the first king's daughter. Here are two kings fighting each other, and one of them in love with the other's daughter, but not saying a word about it.

"Now the second king—the one in love—was not very fierce, and his name was King Muffin—which suggests pleasant thoughts—whereas the first king with the beautiful daughter was called King Odd Zooks, Zooks the Sixth, for he was the sixth of his powerful line. And my story is to show how King Muffin got the better of King Zooks and married his daughter. It was a clever piece of business, for the walls of the castle were high, and the window of the Princess was way above the trees. King Muffin didn't even know which her window was, for it did not have any lace curtains and it looked no better than the cook's, except that the cook sometimes on Monday tied her stockings to the curtain cord to dry. And of course if King Muffin had come openly to the castle, the guards would have cut him all to bits.

"One day in June King Muffin was out on horseback. He had left his crown at home and was wearing his third-best clothes, so you would have thought that he was just an ordinary man. But he was a good horseman; that is, he wasn't thinking every minute about falling off, but sat loosely, as one might sit in a rocking-chair.

"The country was beautiful and green, and in the sky there were puffy clouds that looked the way a pop-over looks before it turns brown—a big pop-over that would stuff even a hungry giant up to his ears. And there was a wind that wiggled everything, and the noise of a brook among the trees. Also, there were birds, but you must not ask me their names, for I am not good at birds.

"King Muffin, although he was a brave man, loved a pleasant day. So he turned back his collar at the throat in order that the wind might tickle his neck and he dropped his reins on his horse's back in a careless way that wouldn't be possible on a street where there were trolley-cars. In this fashion he rode on for several miles and sang to himself a great many songs. Sometimes he knew the words and sometimes he said *tum tum te tum tum,* but he kept to the tune.

"King Muffin enjoyed his ride so much that before he knew it he was out of his own kingdom and at least six parasangs in the kingdom of King Zooks. *My dear, use your handkerchief!*

"And even then King Muffin would not have realized it, except that on turning a corner he saw a young man lying under a tree in a suit that was half green and half yellow. King Muffin knew him at once to be a jester—but whose? King Zooks's jester, of course, his mortal enemy. For jesters have to go off by themselves once in a while to think up new jokes, and no other king lived within riding distance. Really, the jester was thinking of rhymes to *zithern,* which is the name of the curious musical instrument he carried, and is a little like a mandolin, only harder to play. It cannot be learned in twelve easy lessons. And the jester was making a sorry business of it, for it is a difficult word to find rhymes to, as you would know if you tried. He was terribly woeful.

"King Muffin said 'Whoa' and stopped his horse. Then he said 'Good morning, fellow,' in the kind of superior tone that kings use.

"The jester got off the ground and, as he did not know that Muffin was a king, he sneezed; for the ground was damp. It was a slow sneeze in coming, for the ground was not very wet, and he stood waiting for it with his mouth open and his eyes squinting. So King Muffin waited too, and had a moment to think. And as kings think very fast, very many thoughts came to him. So, by the time the sneeze had gone off like a shower bath, and before the pipes filled up for another, some interesting things had occurred to him. Well! things about the Princess and how he might get a chance to speak with her. But he said:

" 'Ho, ho! Methinks King Zooks's jester has the snuffles.'

"At this, Jeppo—for that was the jester's name—looked up with a wry face, for he still kept a sneeze inside him which he couldn't dislodge.

" 'By my boots and spurs!' the King cried again, 'you are a woeful jester.'

"Jeppo *was* woeful. For on this very night King Zooks was to give a grand dinner—not a simple dinner such as you have at home with Annie passing dishes and rattling the pie around the pantry—but a dinner for a hundred persons, generals and ambassadors, all dressed in lace and eating from gold plates.

And of course everyone would look to Jeppo for
something funny—maybe a new song with twenty
verses and a *rol-de-rol-rol chorus,* which everyone
could sing even if he didn't know the words. And
Jeppo didn't know a single new thing. He had tried
to write something, but had stuck while trying to think
of a rhyme for *zithern.* So of course he was woeful.
And King Muffin knew it.

"All this while King Muffin was thinking hard,
although he didn't scowl once, for some persons can
think without scowling. He wished so much to see
the Princess, and yet he knew that if he climbed the
tallest tree he couldn't reach her window. And even
if he found a ladder long enough, as likely as not he
would lean it up against the cook's window, not notic-
ing the stockings on the curtain cord. King Muffin
should have looked glum. But presently he smiled.

"'Jeppo,' he said, 'what would you say if I offered
to change places with you? Here you are fretting
about that song of yours and the dinner only a few
hours off. You will be flogged tomorrow, sure, for
being so dull tonight. Just change clothes with me
and go off and enjoy yourself. Sit in a tavern!
Spend these kywatskies!' Here King Muffin rattled
his pocket. 'I'll take your place. I know a dozen
songs, and they will tickle your king until, goodness
me! he will cry into his soup.' King Muffin really
didn't give King Zooks credit for ordinary manners,
but then he was his mortal enemy, and prej'iced.

"Well, Jeppo *was* terribly woeful and that word

zithern was bothering him. There was *pithern* and *dithern* and *mithern*. He had tried them all, but none of them seemed to mean anything. So he looked at King Muffin, who sat very straight on his horse, for he wasn't at all afraid of him, although he was a tall horse and had nostrils that got bigger and littler all the time; and back legs that twitched. Meanwhile King Muffin twirled a gold chain in his fingers. Then Jeppo looked at King Muffin's clothes and saw that they were fashionable. Then he looked at his hat and there was a yellow feather in it. And those kywat-skies. King Muffin, just to tease him, twirled his moustache, as kings will.

"So the bargain was made. There was a thicket near, so dense that it would have done for taking off your clothes when you go swimming. In this thicket King Muffin and Jeppo exchanged clothes. Of course Jeppo had trouble with the buttons for he had never dressed in such fine clothes before, and many of a king's buttons are behind.

"And now, when the exchange was made, Jeppo inquired where he would find an expensive tavern with brass pull-handles on the lemonade vat, and he rode off, licking his lips and jingling his kywatskies. But King Muffin, dressed as a jester, vaulted on his horse and trotted in the direction of King Zooks's castle, which had indentings around the top like a row of teeth if every other one were pulled.

"And after a little while it became night. It is my private opinion, my dear, which I shall whisper in the

middle of your ear—the outer flap being merely orna-
mental and for 'spection purposes—that the sun is
afraid of the dark, because you never see him around
after nightfall. Bless you, he goes off to bed before
twilight and tucks himself to the chin before you or I
would even think of lighting a candle. And, on my
word, he prefers to sleep in the basement. He goes
down the back stairs and cuddles behind the furnace.
And he has the bad habit, mercy! of reading in bed.
A good half hour after he should be sound asleep, you
can see the reflection of his candle on the evening
clouds."

At this point the old man paused a bit, to see if the
children were still awake. Then he wiped their noses
all around, not forgetting the youngest with the fat
legs, and began again.

"During all this time King Zooks had been getting
ready for the party, trying on shiny coats, and getting
his silk stockings so that the seams at the back went
straight up and didn't wind around, which is the way
they naturally do unless you are particular. And he
put a clean handkerchief into every pocket, in case he
sneezed in a hurry—for King Zooks was a lavish
dresser.

"His wife was dressing in another room, keeping
three maids busy with safety pins and powder-puffs,
and getting all of the snarls out of her hair. And, in
still another room of the castle, his daughter was
dressing. Now his wife was a nice-looking woman,
like nurse, except that she wore stiff brocade and

didn't jounce. But his daughter was beautiful and didn't need a powder-puff.

"When they were all dressed they met outside, just to ask questions of one another about handkerchiefs and noses and behind the ears. The Queen, also, wished to be very sure that there wasn't a hole in the heel of her stocking, for she wore black stockings, which makes it worse. King Zooks was fond of his wife and fond of his daughter, and when he was with them he did not look so fierce. He kissed both of them, but when he kissed his daughter—which was the better fun—he took hold of her nose—but in a most kindly way—so that her face wouldn't slip.

"Then they went down the marble stairs, with flunkies bowing up and down.

"But how worried King Zooks would have been if he had known that at that very moment his enemy, King Muffin, was coming into the castle, disguised as a jester. Nobody stopped King Muffin, for wandering jesters were common in those days.

"And now the party started with all its might.

"King Zooks offered his arm to the wife of the Ambassador, and Queen Zooks offered hers to the General of the army. There was a fight around the Princess, but she said *eenie meenie minie moe, catch a nigger by the toe* and counted them all out but one. And so they went down another marble stairway to the dining-room, where a band was blowing itself red in the face—the trombonist, in particular, seeming to be in great distress.

"And where was King Muffin?

"King Muffin came in by the postern—the back stoop, my dear—and he washed his hands and ears at the kitchen sink and went right up to the dining-room. And there he was standing behind the King's chair, where King Zooks couldn't see him but the Princess could. You can see from this what a crafty person King Muffin was. Queen Zooks, to be sure, could see him, but she was an unsuspicious person, and was very hungry. There were waffles for dinner, and when there were waffles she didn't even talk very much.

"King Muffin was very funny. He told jokes which were old at his own castle, but were new to King Zooks. And King Zooks, thinking he was a real jester, laughed until he cried—only his tears did not get into his soup, for by that time the soup had been cleared away. A few of them, however—just a splatter—did fall on his fish, but it didn't matter as it was a salt fish anyway. But all the guests, inasmuch as they were eating away from home, had to be more particular. And when the *rol-de-rol-rol* choruses came, how King Zooks sang, throwing back his head and forgetting all about his ferocious moustache!

"No one enjoyed the fun more than King Muffin. Whenever things quieted down a bit he said something even funnier than the last. But during all this time it had not occurred to King Zooks to inquire for Jeppo, or to ask why a new fool stood behind his chair. He just laughed and nudged the wife of the Ambassador with his elbow and ate his waffles and enjoyed himself.

"So the dinner grew merrier and merrier until at last everyone had had enough to eat. They would have pushed back a little from the table to be more comfortable in front, except for their manners. King Zooks was the last to finish, for the dinner ended with ice-cream and he was fond of it. He didn't have it ordinary days. In fact he was so eager to get the last bit that he scraped his spoon round and round upon the dish until Queen Zooks was ashamed of him. When, finally, he was all through, the guests folded their napkins and pushed back their chairs until you never heard such a squeak. A few of them—but these had never been out to dinner before—had spilled crumbs in their laps and had to brush them off.

"And now there was a dance.

"So King Zooks offered his arm to the wife of the Ambassador and Queen Zooks offered hers to the General of the army, and they started up the marble stairway to the ballroom. But what should King Muffin do but skip up to the Princess while she was still smoothing out her skirts. (Yellow organdie, my dear, and it musses when you sit on it.) Muffin made a low bow and kissed her hand. Then he asked her for the first dance. It was so preposterous that a jester should ask her to dance at all, that everyone said it was the funniest thing he had done, and they went into a gale about it on the marble stairway. Even Queen Zooks, who ordinarily didn't laugh much

at jokes, threw back her head and laughed quite loud
—but in a minute, when everybody else was done.
And then to everyone's surprise the Princess con-
sented to dance with King Muffin, although the General of the army stood by in a kind of empty fashion.
But everybody was so merry, and in particular King
Zooks, that no one minded.

"King Muffin, when he danced with the Princess,
looked at her very hard and softly, and she looked
back at him as if she didn't mind it a bit. Evidently
she knew him despite his disguise. And naturally she
knew that he was in love with her.

"Now King Muffin hadn't had a thing to eat, for
jesters are supposed to eat at a little table afterwards.
If they ate at the big table they would forget and sing
sometimes with their mouths full and you know how
that would sound. So he and the Princess went downstairs to the pantry, where he ate seven cream puffs
and three floating islands, one after the other, never
spilling a bit on his blouse. He called them 'floatin'
Irelands,' having learned it that way as a child, his
nurse not correcting him. Then he felt better and they
returned to the ballroom, where the dance was still
going on with all its might.

"King Muffin took the Princess out on the balcony,
which was the place where young gentlemen, even in
those days, took ladies when they had something particular to say. He shut the door carefully and looked
all around to make sure that there were no spies about,
under the chairs, inside the vases. He even wiggled

the rug for fear that there might be a trapdoor
beneath.

"Did the Princess love King Muffin? Of course
she did. But she wasn't going to let him know it all
at once. Ladies never do things like that. So she
looked indifferent, as though she might yawn at any
moment. Despite that, King Muffin told her what
was on his mind, and when he was finished, he looked
for an answer. But she didn't say anything, but just
sat quiet and pretended there was a button off her
dress. So King Muffin told it again, and moved up a
bit. And this time her head nodded ever so little. But
he saw it. So he reached down in his side pocket, so
far that he had to straighten out his leg to get to the
bottom. He brought up a ring. Then he slipped it
on her finger, the next to the longest one on her left
hand. After that he kissed her in a most affectionate
way.

"This was all very well, but of course King Zooks
would never consent to their marriage. And if he
discovered that the new jester was King Muffin, his
guards would cut him all to slivers. For a minute
they were woeful. Then a bright idea came to King
Muffin—

"Meanwhile the dance had been going on with all
its might. First the General of the army danced with
Queen Zooks. He was a very manly dancer and was
quite stiff from the waist up, and she bounced around
on tip-toe. Then the Ambassador danced with her,
but his sword kept getting in her way. Then both of

them, having done their duty, looked around for the Princess. They went to the lemonade room, for that was the first place naturally to look. Then they went to the cardroom, where the older persons were playing casino, and were sitting very solemn, as if it were not a party at all.

"Then they went to King Zooks, who was jiggling on his toes, with his back to the fire, full and happy. 'Where is your daughter, Majestical Majesty?' they asked. But as King Zooks didn't know he joined the search, and Queen Zooks, too. But she wasn't much good at it, for she had a long train and she couldn't turn a corner sharp, although her maids trotted after her and whisked it about as fast as possible.

"But they couldn't find the Princess anywhere inside the castle.

"After a while it occurred to King Zooks that the cook might know. She had gone to bed—leaving her dishes until morning—so up they climbed. She answered from under the covers, 'Whajuwant?' which shows that she didn't talk English and was probably a Spanish cook or an Indian princess captured very young. So she got up, all excited. My! how she scuffed around, looking for her slippers, trying to find her clothes and getting one or two things on wrong side out! She was so confused that she thought it was morning and brushed her teeth.

"By this time an hour had passed and King Zooks was fidgety. He told his red-faced band to lean their trombones and other things up against the wall, so that he could think. Then he stroked his chin, while the court stood by and tried to think also. Finally the King sent a herald to proclaim around the castle how fidgety he was and that his daughter must be brought to him. But the Princess was not found. Meantime the band ate ice-cream and cocoanut macaroons, and appeared to enjoy itself.

"In a tall tower that stands high above the trees there was a great clock, and, by and by, it began to strike the hour. It did not stop until it had struck ten times. So you see it was growing late and the King had the right to be getting fidgety. When the clock had done, those guests who were not in the habit of sitting up so late, began to grow sleepy; only, of course, they did not yawn out loud, but behind fans and things.

"Meanwhile King Muffin had gone downstairs to the stable. He brought out his horse with the flaring nostrils and another horse also. He took them around to the Princess, who sat waiting for him on a marble bench in the shadow of a tree.

" 'Climb up, beautiful Princess,' he said.

"She hopped into her saddle and he into his. They were off like the wind.

"They heard the clock strike ten and they saw the great tower rising above the castle with the silver moon upon it, but they galloped on and on. Through the forest they galloped, over bridges and streams. And the moon climbed off the tower and kept with them—as it does with all good folk—plunging through the clouds like a ship upon the ocean. And still they galloped on. Presently they met Jeppo returning from the tavern with the brass pull-handles. 'Yo, ho!' called out the King, and they passed him in a flash. *Clackety-clack-clack, clackety-clack-clack, clack-clack, clackety-clack!*

"And peasants, who usually slept right through the night, awoke at the sound of their hoofs and although they were very sleepy, they ran and looked out of their windows—being careful to put on slippers so as not to get the snuffles. And King Muffin and the Princess galloped by with the moonlight upon them, and the peasants wondered who they were. But as they were very sleepy, presently they went back to bed without finding out. One of them did, however, stumble against a chair, right on the toe, and had to light a candle to see if it were worth mending.

"But in the morning the peasants found a bauble near the lodge-gate, a cap and bells on the ravine bridge, and on the long road to the border of King Muffin's land they found a jester's coat.

"And to this day, although many years have passed, their children and their children's children, on the way from school, gather the lilies of the valley which flourish in the woods and along the roads. And they think that they are jesters' bells which were scattered in the flight."

Whereupon the old man, having finished his story, wiped the noses of the children, not forgetting the youngest one with the fat legs, and sent them off to bed.

The Crowded Curb.

RECENTLY I came on an urchin in the crowded city, pitching pennies by himself, in the angle of an abutment. Three feet from his patched seat—a gay pattern which he tilted upward now and then—there moved a thick stream of shoppers. He was in solitary contest with himself, his evening papers neglected in a heap, wrapped in his score, unconscious of the throng that pressed against him. He was resting from labor, as a greater merchant takes to golf for his refreshment. The curb was his club. He had fetched his recreation down to business, to the vacancy between editions. Presently he will scoop his earnings to his pocket and will bawl out to his advantage our latest murder.

How mad—how delightful our streets would be if all of us followed as unreservedly, with so little self-consciousness or respect of small convention, our innocent desires!

Who of us even whistles in a crowd?—or in the spring goes with a skip and leap?

A lady of my acquaintance—who grows plump in her early forties—tells me that she has always wanted to run after an ice-wagon and ride up town, bouncing on the tail-board. It is doubtless an inheritance from a childhood which was stifled and kept in starch. A singer, also, of bellowing bass, has confided to me

that he would like above all things to roar his tunes
down town on a crowded crossing.   The trolley-cars,
he feels, the motors and all the shrill instruments of
traffic, are no more than a sufficient orchestra for his
lusty upper register.   An old lady, too, in the daintiest
of lace caps, with whom I lately sat at dinner, confessed that whenever she has seen hop-scotch chalked
in an eddy of the crowded city, she has been tempted
to gather up her skirts and join the play.

But none of these folk obey their instinct.   Opinion
chills them.   They plod the streets with gray exterior.
Once, on Fifth Avenue, to be sure, when it was barely
twilight, I observed a man, suddenly, without warning, perform a cart-wheel, heels over head.   He was
dressed in the common fashion.   Surely he was not
an advertisement.   He bore no placard on his hat.
Nor was it apparent that he practiced for a circus.
Rather, I think, he was resolved for once to let the
stiff, censorious world go by unheeded, and be himself
alone.

On a night of carnival how greedily the crowd
assumes the pantaloon!   A day that was prim and
solemn at the start now dresses in cap and bells.   How
recklessly it stretches its charter for the broadest jest!
Observe those men in women's bonnets!   With what
delight they swing their merry bladders at the crowd!
They are hard on forty.   All week they have bent to
their heavy desks, but tonight they take their pay of
life.   The years are a sullen garment, but on a night
of carnival they toss it off.   Blood that was cold and

temperate at noon now feels the fire. Scratch a man
and you find a clown inside. It was at the celebration
of the Armistice that I followed a sober fellow for a
mile, who beat incessantly with a long iron spoon on
an ash-can top. Almost solemnly he advanced among
the throng. Was it joy entirely for the ending of the
war? Or rather was he not yielding at last to an old
desire to parade and be a band? The glad occasion
merely loosed him from convention. That lady friend
of mine, in the circumstance, would have bounced on
ice-wagons up to midnight.

For it is convention, rather than our years—it is the
respect and fear of our neighbors that restrains us on
an ordinary occasion. If we followed our innocent
desires at the noon hour, without waiting for a carnival, how mad our streets would seem! The bellowing
bass would pitch back his head and lament the fair
Isolde. The old lady in lace cap would tuck up her
skirts for hop-scotch and score her goal at last.

Is it not the French who set aside a special night
for foolery, when everyone appears in fancy costume?
They should set the celebration forward in the day,
and let the blazing sun stare upon their mirth. Merriment should not wait upon the owl.

The Dickey Club at Harvard, I think, was fash-
ioned with some such purpose of release. Its initia-
tion occurs always in the spring, when the blood of
an undergraduate is hottest against restraint. It is
a vent placed where it is needed most. Zealously
the candidates perform their pranks. They exceed

the letter of their instruction. The streets of Boston
are a silly spectacle. Young men wear their trousers
inside out and their coats reversed. They greet
strangers with preposterous speech. I once came on
a merry fellow eating a whole pie with great mouth-
fuls on the Court House steps, explaining meantime
to the crowd that he was the youngest son of Little
Jack Horner. And, of course, with such a hardened
gourmand for an ancestor, he was not embarrassed by
his ridiculous posture.

But it is not youth which needs the stirring most.
Nor need one necessarily play an absurd antic to be
natural. And therefore, here at home, on our own
Soldiers' Monument—on its steps and pediment that
mount above the street—I offer a few suggestions to
the throng.

Ladies and gentlemen! I invite you to a carnival.
Here! Now! At noon! I bid you to throw off your
solemn pretense. And be yourself! That sober
manner is a cloak. Your dignity scarcely reaches to
your skin. Does no one desire to play leap-frog
across those posts? Do none of you care to skip and
leap? What! Will no one accept my invitation?

You, my dear sirs, I know you. You play chess
together every afternoon in your club. One of you
carries at this moment a small board in his waistcoat
pocket. Why hurry to your club, gentlemen? Here
on this step is a place to play your game. Surely your
concentration is proof against the legs that swing
around you. And you, my dear sir! I see that you

are a scholar by your bag of books. You chafe for your golden studies. Come, sit alongside! Here is a shady spot for the pursuit of knowledge. Did not Socrates ply his book in the public concourse?

My dear young lady, it is evident that a desire has seized you to practice your soprano voice. Why do you wait for your solitary piano to pitch the tune? On these steps you can throw your trills up heavenward.

An ice-wagon! With a tail-board! Is there no lady in her forties, prim in youth, who will take her fling? Or does no gentleman in silk hat wish a piece of ice to suck?

Observe that good-natured father with his son! They have shopped for toys. He carries a bundle beneath his arm. It is doubtless a mechanical bear— a creature that roars and walks on the turning of a key. After supper these two will squat together on the parlor carpet and wind it up for a trial performance. But must such an honest pleasure sit for the coming of the twilight? Break the string! Insert the key! Let the fearful creature stride boldly among the shoppers.

Here is an iron balustrade along the steps. A dozen of you desire, secretly, to slide down its slippery length.

My dear madam, it is plain that the heir is naughty. Rightfully you have withdrawn his lollypop. And now he resists your advance, stiff-legged and spunky. Your stern eye already has passed its sentence. You merely wait to get him home. I offer you these steps in lieu of nursery or woodshed. You have only to tip him up. Surely the flat of your hand gains no cunning by delay.

And you, my dear sir—you who twirl a silk moustache—you with the young lady on your arm! If I am not mistaken you will woo your fair companion on this summer evening beneath the moon. Must so good a deed await the night? Shall a lover's arms hang idle all the day? On these steps, my dear sir, a kiss, at least, may be given as a prelude.

Hop-scotch! Where is my old friend of the lace cap? The game is already chalked upon the stones.

Is there no one in the passing throng who desires to dance? Are there no toes that wriggle for release? My dear lady, the rhythmic swish of your skirt betrays you. A tune for a merry waltz runs through your head. Come! we'll find you a partner in the crowd. Those silk stockings of yours must not be wasted in a mincing gait.

Have lawyers, walking sourly on their business, any sweeter nature to display to us? Our larger merchants seem covered with restraint and thought of profit. That physician with his bag of pellets seems not to know that laughter is a panacea. Has Labor no desire to play leap-frog on its pick and go shouting home to supper? Housewives follow their unfaltering noses from groceries to meats. Will neither gingham nor brocade romp and cut a caper for us?

Ladies and gentlemen! Why wait for a night of carnival? Does not the blood flow red, also, at the noon hour? Must the moon point a silly finger before you start your merriment? I offer you these steps.

Is there no one who will whistle in the crowd? Will none of you, even in the spring, go with a skip and leap upon your business?

A Corner for Echoes.

SOMETIMES in a quiet hour I see in the memory of my childhood a frame house across a wide lawn from a pleasant street. There are no trees about the yard, in itself a defect, yet in its circumstance, as the house arises in my view, the barrenness denotes no more than a breadth of sunlight across those endless days.

There was, indeed, in contrast and by way of shadowy admonishment, a church near by, whose sober bell, grieving lest our joy should romp too long, recalled us to fearful introspection on Sunday evening, and it moved me chiefly to the thought of eternity—eternity everlasting. Reward or punishment mattered not. It was Time itself that plagued me, Time that rolled like a wheel forever until the imagination reeled

and sickened. And on Thursday evening also—
another bad intrusion on the happy week—again
the sexton tugged at the rope for prayer and the
dismal clapper answered from above. It is strange
that a man in friendly red suspenders, pipe in mouth
as he pushed his lawn-mower through the week, should
spread such desolation. But presently, when our
better neighbors were stiffly gathered in and had composed their skirts, a brisker hymn arose. Tenor and
soprano assured one another vigorously from pew to
pew that they were Christian soldiers marching as to
war. When they were off at last for the fair Jerusalem, the fret of eternity passed from me. And yet,
for the most part, we played in sunlight all the week,
and our thoughts dwelt happily on wide horizons.

There was another church, far off across the house-
tops, seen only from an attic window, whose bells in
contrast were of a pleasant jangle. Exactly where
this church stood I never knew. Its towers arose
above a neighbor's barn and acknowledged no base or
local habitation. Indeed, its glittering and unsub-
stantial spire offered a hint that it was but an imaginary creature of the attic, a pageant that mustered
only to the view of him who looked out through these
narrow, cobwebbed windows. For here, as in a kind
of magic, the twilight flourished at the noon and its
shadows practiced beforehand for the night. Through
these windows children saw the unfamiliar, distant
marvels of the world—towers and kingdoms unseen

by older eyes that were grown dusty with common sights.

Yet regularly, out of a noonday stillness—except for the cries of the butcher boy upon the steps—a dozen clappers of the tower struck their sudden din across the city. It appeared that at the very moment of the noon, having lagged to the utmost second, the frantic clappers had bolted up the belfry stairs to call the town to dinner. Or perhaps to an older ear their discordant and heterodox tongue hinted that Roman infallibility had here fallen into argument and that various and contrary doctrine was laboring in warm dispute. Certainly the clappers were brawling in the tower and had come to blows. But a half mile off it was an agreeable racket and did not rouse up eternity to tease me.

Across from our house, but at the rear, with only an alley entrance, there was a building in which pies were baked—a horrid factory in our very midst!—and insolent smoke curled off the chimney and flaunted our imperfection. Respectable ladies, long resident, wearing black poke bonnets and camel's-hair shawls, lifted their patrician eyebrows with disapproval. Scorn sat on their gentle up-turned noses. They held their skirts close, in passing, from contamination. These pies could not count upon their patronage. They were contraband even in a pinch, with unexpected guests arrived. It were better to buy of Cobey, the grocer on the Circle. And the building did smell heavily of its commodity. But despite detraction, as one came from school, when the wind was north, an agreeable whiff of lard and cooking touched the nostrils as a happy prologue to one's dinner. Sometimes a cart issued to the street, boarded close, full of pies on shelves, and rattled cityward.

The fire station was around the corner and down a hill. We marveled at the polished engine, the harness that hung ready from the ceiling, the poles down which the firemen slid from their rooms above. It was at the fire station that we got the baseball score, inning by inning, and other news, if it was worthy, from the outside world. But perhaps we dozed in a hammock or were lost with Oliver Optic in a jungle when the fire-bell rang. If spry, we caught a glimpse of the hook-and-ladder from the top of the hill, or the horses galloping up the slope. But would none of our neighbors ever burn? we thought. Must all candles be overturned far off?

Near the school-house was the reservoir, a mound and pond covering all the block. Round about the top there was a gravel path that commanded the city— the belching chimneys on the river, the ships upon the lake, and to the south a horizon of wooded hills. The world lay across that tumbled ridge and there our thoughts went searching for adventure. Perhaps these were the foothills of the Himalaya and from the top were seen the towers of Babylon. Perhaps there was an ocean, with white sails which were blown from the Spanish coast. On a summer afternoon clouds drifted across the sky, like mountains on a journey—emigrants, they seemed, from a loftier range, seeking a fresh plain on which to erect their fortunes.

But the chief use of this reservoir, except for its wholly subsidiary supply of water, was its grassy slope. It was usual in the noon recess—when we were cramped with learning—to slide down on a barrel stave and be wrecked and spilled midway. In default of stave a geography served as sled, for by noon the most sedentary geography itched for action. Of what profit—so it complained—is a knowledge of the world if one is cooped always with stupid primers in a desk? Of what account are the boundaries of Hindostan, if one is housed all day beneath a lid with slate and pencils? But the geography required an exact balance, with feet lifted forward into space, and with fingers gripped behind. Our present geographies, alas, are of smaller surface, and, unless students have shrunk and shriveled, their more profitable use upon a hill is past. Some children descended without stave or book, and their preference was marked upon their shining seats.

It was Hoppy who marred this sport. Hoppy was the keeper of the reservoir, a one-legged Irishman with a crutch. His superfluous trouser-leg was folded and pinned across, and it was a general quarry for patches. When his elbow or his knees came through, here was a remedy at hand. Here his wife clipped, also, for her crazy quilt. And all the little Hoppies— for I fancy him to have been a family man—were rein-

forced from this extra cloth. But when Hoppy's bad
profile appeared at the top of the hill we grabbed our
staves and scurried off. The cry of warning—"Peg-
leg's a-comin' "—still haunts my memory. It was
Hoppy's reward to lead one of us smaller fry roughly
by the ear. Or he gripped us by the wrist and snapped
his stinging finger at our nose. Then he pitched us
through the fence where a wooden slat was gone.

Hoppy's crutch was none of your elaborate affairs,
curved and glossy. Instead, it was only a stout, un-
varnished stick, with a padded cross-piece at the top.
But the varlet could run, leaping forward upon us
with long, uneven strides. And I have wondered
whether Stevenson, by any chance, while he was still
pondering the plot of "Treasure Island," may not
have visited our city and, seeing Hoppy on our heels,
have contrived John Silver out of him. He must have
built him anew above the waist, shearing him at his
suspender buttons, scrapping his common upper parts;
but the wooden stump and breeches were a precious
salvage. His crutch, at the least, became John
Silver's very timber.

The Circle was down the street. In the center of
this sunny park there arose an artificial mountain,
with a waterfall that trickled off the rocks pleasantly
on hot days. Ruins and blasted towers, battlements
and cement grottoes, were still the fashion. In those
days masons built stony belvederes and laid pipes
which burst forth into mountain pools a good ten feet
above the sidewalk. The cliff upon our Circle, with

its path winding upward among the fern, its tiny
castle on the peak and its tinkle of little water, sprang
from this romantic period. From the terrace on top
one could spit over the balustrade on the unsuspecting
folk who walked below. Later the town had a mechanical ship that sailed around the pond. As often
as this ship neared the cliffs the mechanical captain on
the bridge lifted his glasses with a startled jerk and
gave orders for the changing of the course.

Tinkey's shop was on the Circle. One side of
Tinkey's window was a bakery with jelly-cakes and
angel-food. This, as I recall, was my earliest theology.
Heaven, certainly, was worth the effort. The other
window unbent to peppermint sticks and grab-bags to
catch our dirtier pennies. But this meaner produce
was a concession to the trade, and the Tinkey fingers,
from father down to youngest daughter, touched it
with scorn. Mrs. Tinkey, in particular, who, we
thought, was above her place, lifted a grab-bag at
arm's length, and her nostrils quivered as if she held
a dead mouse by the tail.

But in the essence Tinkey was a caterer and his
handiwork was shown in the persons of a frosted bride
and groom who waited before a sugar altar for the
word that would make them man and wife. Her nose
in time was bruised—a careless lifting of the glass by
the youngest Miss Tinkey—but he, like a faithful
suitor, stood to his youthful pledge.

Beyond the shop was a room with blazing red wall
paper and a fiery carpet. In this hot furnace, out-

rivaling the boasts of Abednego, the neighborhood perspired pleasantly on August nights, and ate ice-cream. If we arose to the price of a Tinkey layer-cake thick with chocolate, the night stood out in splendor above its fellows.

Around the corner was Conrad's bookstore. Conrad was a dumpy fellow with unending good humor and a fat, soft hand. He sometimes called lady customers, *My dear,* but it was only in his eagerness to press a sale. I do not recall that he was a scholar. If you asked to be shown the newest books, he might offer you the "Vicar of Wakefield" as a work just off the press, and tell you that Goldsmith was a man to watch. A young woman assistant read The Duchess between customers. In her fancy she eloped daily with a duke, but actually she kept company with a grocer's clerk. They ate sodas together at Tinkey's. How could he know, poor fellow, when their fingers met beneath the table, that he was but a substitute in her high romance? At the very moment, in her thoughts, she was off with the duke beneath the moon. Conrad had also an errand boy with a dirty face, who spent the day on a packing case at the rear of the shop, where he ate an endless succession of apples. An orchard went through him in the season.

Conrad's shop was only moderate in books, but it spread itself in fancy goods—crackers for the Fourth —marbles and tops in their season—and for Saint Valentine's Day a range of sentiment that distanced his competitors. A lover, though he sighed like furnace, found here mottoes for his passion. Also there were "comics"—base insulting valentines of suitable greeting from man to man. These were three for a nickel just as they came off the pile, but two for a nickel with selection.

At Christmas, Conrad displayed china inkstands. There was one of these which, although often near a sale, still stuck to the shelves year after year. The beauty of its device dwelt in a little negro who perched at the rear on a rustic fence that held the penholders. But suddenly, when choice was wavering in his favor, off he would pitch into the inkwell. At this mischance Conrad would regularly be astonished, and he would sell instead a china camel whose back was hollowed out for ink. Then he laved the negro for the twentieth time and set him back upon the fence, where he sat like an interrupted suicide with his dark eye again upon the pool.

Nor must I forget a line of Catholic saints. There was one jolly bit of crockery—Saint Patrick, I believe —that had lost an arm. This defect should have been considered a further mark of piety—a martyrdom unrecorded by the church—a special flagellation—but although the price in successive years sunk to thirty-nine and at last to the wholly ridiculous sum of twenty-three cents—less than one third the price of his unbroken but really inferior mates (Saint Aloysius and Saint Anthony)—yet he lingered on.

Nowhere was there a larger assortment of odd and unmatched letter paper. No box was full and many were soiled. If pink envelopes were needed, Conrad, unabashed, laid out a blue, or with his fat thumb he fumbled two boxes into one to complete the count. Initialed paper once had been the fashion—G for Gladys—and there was still a remnant of several letters toward the end of the alphabet. If one of these chanced to fit a customer, with what zest Conrad blew upon the box and slapped it! But until Xenophon and Xerxes shall come to buy, these final letters must rest unsold upon his shelves.

Conrad was a dear good fellow (Bless me! he is still alive—just as fat and bow-legged, with the same soft hand, just as friendly!) and when he retired at last from business the street lost half its mirth and humor.

Near Conrad's shop and the Circle was our house. By it a horse-car jangled, one way only, cityward, at intervals of twelve minutes. In winter there was straw on the floor. In front was a fare-box with sliding shelves down which the nickels rattled, or, if one's memory lagged, the thin driver rapped his whip-handle on the glass. He sat on a high stool which was padded to eke out nature.

Once before, as I have read, there was a corner for echoes. The buildings were set so that the quiet folk who dwelt near by could hear the sound of coming steps—steps far off, then nearer until they tramped beneath the windows. Then, as they listened, the sounds faded. And it seemed to him who chronicled the place that he heard the persons of his drama

coming—little steps that would grow to manhood,
steps that faltered already toward their final curtain.
But there is no plot to thicken around our corner. Or
rather, there are a hundred plots. And when I listen
in fancy to the echoes, I hear the general tapping of
our neighbors—beloved feet that have gone into darkness for a while.

I hear the footsteps of an old man. When he trod
our street he was of gloomy temper. The world was
awry for him. He was sunk in despair at politics, yet
I recall that he relished an apple. As often as he
stopped to see us, he told us that the country had gone
to the demnition bow-wows, and he snapped at his
apple as if it had been a Democrat. His little dog
ran a full block ahead of him on their evening stroll,
and always trotted into our gateway. He sat on the
lowest step with his eyes down the street. "Master,"
he seemed to say, "here we all are, waiting for you."

John Smith cut the grass on the Circle. He was a
friend of children, and, for his nod and greeting, I
drove down street my span of tin horses on a wheel.
Hand in hand we climbed his rocky mountain to see
where the waterfall spurted from a pipe. Below, the
neighbors' bonnets, with baskets, went to shop at
Cobey's. I still hear the click of his lawn-mower of
a summer afternoon.

Darky Dan beat our carpets. He was a merry
fellow and he sang upon the street. Wild melodies
they were, with head thrown back and crazy laughter.
He was a harmless, good-natured fellow, but nurse-

maids huddled us close until his song had turned the corner.

I recall a crippled child—maybe of half wit only— who dragged a broken foot. To our shame he seemed a comic creature and we pelted him with snowballs and ran from his piteous anger.

A match-boy with red hair came by on winter nights and was warmed beside the fire. My father questioned him—as one merchant to another—about his business, and mother kept him in mittens. In payment for bread and jam he loosed his muffler and played the mouth-organ. In turn we blew upon the vents, but as music it was naught. Gone is that melody. The house is dark.

There was an old lady lived near by in almost feudal state. Her steps were the broadest on the street, her walnut doors were carved in the deepest pattern, her fence was the highest. Her furniture, the year around, was covered in linen cloths, and the great chairs with their claw feet resembled the horses in panoply that draw the chariot of the Nubian Queen in the circus parade. With this old lady there lived an old cook, an old second-maid, an old laundress and an old coachman. The second-maid thrust a platter at you as you sat at table and nudged you in the ribs— if you were a child—"Eat it," she said, "it's good!" The coachman nodded on his box, the laundress in her tubs, but the cook was spry despite her years. In the yard there was a fountain—all yards had fountains then—and I used to wonder whether this were the font of Ponce de León that restored the aged to their youth. Here, surely, was the very house to test the cure. And when the ancient laundress came by I speculated whether, after a sudden splash, she would emerge a dazzling princess.

With this old lady there dwelt a niece, or a daughter, or a younger sister—relationship was vague —and this niece owned a little black dog. But the old lady was dull of sight and in the dark passages of her house she waved her arm and kept saying, "Whisk, Nigger! Whisk, Nigger!" for she had stepped once on the creature's tail. Every year she gave a children's party, and we youngsters looked for magic in a mirror and went to Jerusalem around her solemn chairs. She had bought toys and trinkets from Europe for all of us.

Then there was an old neighbor, a justice of the peace, who, being devoid of much knowledge of the law, put his cases to my grandfather. When he had been advised, he stroked his beard and said it was an opinion to which he had come himself. He went down the steps mumbling the judgment to keep it in his memory.

It was my grandfather's custom in the late afternoon of summer, when the sun had slanted, to pull a chair off the veranda and sit sprinkling the lawn with his crutch beside him. Toward supper Mr. Hodge, a building contractor and our neighbor, went by. His wagon usually rattled with some bit of salvage—perhaps an iron bath-tub plucked from a building before he wrecked it, or a kitchen sink. His yard was piled with the fruitage of his profession. Mr. Hodge was of sociable turn and he cried *whoa* to his jogging horse.

Now ensued a half-hour's gossip. It was the comedy of the occasion that the horse, after having made several attempts to start and been stopped by a jerking of the reins, took to craftiness. He put forward a hoof, quite carelessly it seemed. If there was no protest, in time he tried a diagonal hoof behind. It was then but a shifting of the weight to swing forward a step. "Whoa!" yelled Mr. Hodge. "Yes, yes," the old horse seemed to answer, "certainly, of course, yes, yes! But can't a fellow shift his legs?" In this way the sly brute inched toward supper. My grandfather enjoyed this comedy, and once, if I am not mistaken, I caught him exchanging a wink with the horse. Certainly the beast was glancing round to find a partner for his jest. A conversation, begun at the standpipe, progressed to the telegraph pole, and at last came opposite the kitchen. As my grandfather did not move his chair, Mr. Hodge lifted his voice until the neighborhood knew the price of brick and the unworthiness of plumbers. Mr. Hodge was a Republican and he spoke in favor of the tariff. To clinch an argument he had a usual formula. "It's neither here nor there," and he brought his fist against the dashboard, *"it's right here."* But finally the hungry horse prevailed, Mr. Hodge slapped the reins in consent and they rattled home to supper.

Around this corner, also, there are echoes of chil-

dren's feet—racing feet upon the grass—feet that lag
in the morning on the way to school and run back at
four o'clock—feet that leap the hitching posts or avoid
the sidewalk cracks. Girls' feet rustle in the fallen
leaves, and they think their skirts are silk. And I hear
dimly the cries of hide-and-seek and pull-away and the
merriment of blindman's buff. One lad rises in my
memory who won our marbles. Another excelled us
all when he threw his top. His father was a grocer
and we envied him his easy access to the candy counter.

And particularly I remember a little girl with
yellow curls and blue eyes. She was the Sleeping
Beauty in a Christmas play. I had known her before
in daytime gingham and I had judged her to be as
other girls—creatures that tag along and spoil the
fun. But now, as she rested in laces for the picture,
she dazzled my imagination; for I was the silken
Prince to awaken her. For a week I wished to run
to sea, sink a pirate ship, and be worthy of her love.
But then a sewer was dug along the street and I was
a miner instead—recusant to love—digging in the
yellow sand for the center of the earth.

But chiefly it is the echo of older steps I hear—
steps whose sound is long since stilled—feet that have
crossed the horizon and have gone on journey for a
while. And when I listen I hear echoes that are
fading into silence.